COMMUNICATION SERIES

Keith Evans

Common Sense Rules of Advocacy
for Lawyers

for Lawyers

TheCapitol.Net

TheCapitol.Net, Inc. is a non-partisan firm offering training and information for government and business leaders that strengthens representative government and the rule of law. TheCapitol.Net is the exclusive provider of Congressional Quarterly Executive Conferences.

We publish practical, hands-on works for practitioners, written by subject matter experts. If you want to teach or write for practitioners in law, business, or government affairs, we would like to talk with you.

Our products and services can be found on our website at www.TheCapitol.Net

Additional copies of *Common Sense Rules of Advocacy for Lawyers* can be ordered directly from the publisher. Secure online ordering is available on the website: www.RulesOfAdvocacy.com

Production and prepress by Zaccarine Design, Evanston, IL 847-864-3994.

Evans, Keith, 1936-
    Common sense rules of advocacy for lawyers / by Keith Evans.
    p. cm. -- (Communication series)
    Includes index.
    Rev. ed. of: The common sense rules of trial advocacy.
  St. Paul, Minn. : West Pub. Co., 1994.
    LCCN 2003113147
    ISBN 1587330059

    1. Trial practice--United States. I. Evans, Keith.
    1936-Common sense rules of trial advocacy. II. Title.

    KF8915.E95 2004   347.73'75
                    QBI03-200894

Foreword

I wrote this book in the first place* as a kind of guidebook for young lawyers who had to do a trial in court. And I have been pleased over the years to hear from people who claimed they had won a verdict because they used one of the techniques I suggested. I have been told as well that these practical rules are as useful outside the courtroom as they are in it. And I do agree that if you have to make a presentation or negotiate a deal, these rules will undoubtedly help you.

But I don't want to re-write the book so as to point out that this or that rule is of particular importance in any kind of negotiation or alternative dispute resolution, or that an account executive making a pitch should pay special attention to this one or that one. You are intelligent enough to see how a rule lifts out of the courtroom and can be used in negotiations and presentations, and, indeed, in every kind of relationship. My second wife complained, "I wish you'd use your advocacy on me," and looking back on it, I should have done.

And it is in the framework of a trial in court that the rules can be most easily explained. So although I have been persuaded to adopt a new title, what you are getting here is more or less the original advice for the brave young lawyers who dare to do a case in court. You'll find it quite funny in places, and you'll easily decide which rules you want to take with you into your daily life and into your work.

I think the central rule of this whole book is Newton's Rule, as I have called it. "You can't possibly convict my client on this evidence," says the lawyer, and although the jury don't move a muscle you can see them all thinking, "Oh no? You wanna bet?" Every action has its equal and opposite reaction, and this rule is working all the time when people are communicating or trying to communicate.

But we'll come to Newton's Rule, as we will to the Rule of the Honest Guide. When you've familiarized yourself with all the rules you'll even find it easier to fix a date.

If a new rule occurs to you and you are willing to share it, please get in touch and tell me about it. I can be contacted through my publisher, Chug Roberts, at TheCapitol.Net, PO Box 25706, Alexandria, VA 22313-5706; www.TheCapitol.Net; 202-678-1600, and I very much look forward to seeing this collection added to.

Here, then, apart from the occasional footnote, is the book as it was designed for the lawyers. Enjoy—as they intransitively say in California.

Keith Evans
February 2004

---

* This book was originally published in 1994 by West Publishing as "The Common Sense Rules of Trial Advocacy." Appendix Three, "How to Succeed as a Lawyer," by Roland Boyd, is new in this edition.

Original Foreword

(December, 1993)

This book is based upon a seminar which has been presented in many parts of America under the sponsorship of the American Inns of Court Foundation. Since the American Inn of Court is a comparatively new arrival on the scene, a word of explanation is called for.

The original Inns of Court in London came into being in the 1300s, and for centuries they have been centers of training for English-speaking trial lawyers. Before the Revolutionary War many Americans studied there: several of the people who signed the Declaration of Independence were members of those original Inns of Court. But after 1776, America went its own way and unified its legal profession, doing away with the ancient distinction between specialist trial lawyers and the rest.

No harm was done by this. On the contrary, American trial advocacy went from strength to strength during the 200 years that followed and produced some of the finest advocates in the history of the English language. But then came the explosion of the discovery.

Young men and women who had come to the bar, fired with the ambition to spellbind juries, found that, instead, they were having to spend their time taking or defending depositions and treading the paper-mill. They hardly got into court at all and had to wait years for their first trials. The bench began to complain about falling standards, and about what one distinguished judge called "the proliferation of incompetents in the courts." In hardly more than one generation, the effective, courteous, economical, entertaining advocate became almost an endangered species. Out of the need to do something about this came the idea of the American Inn of Court.

What happened was remarkable. A federal judge called together the leading trial lawyers of his district and, with the authority of his office, there and then created a kind of club, a society surprisingly like one of the old Inns of Court. Here the best trial lawyers of the older generation could meet regularly with much younger attorneys and try to pass on the trial skills, the ethics, and the courtesy learned in a lifetime of trial practice. The younger lawyers were accepted as members of the Inn for a limited period, while the senior attorneys, and many judges as well, committed to several years of meeting and teaching. The entire membership met once a month for a few intensive hours, and twice a year they all sat down together at a formal dinner. One intake of young lawyers was succeeded by the next, and the influence of this new, American Inn of Court steadily spread out through the community.

It also spread throughout the country. In 1993, as this book goes to press, there are already more than 200 Inns across America*. Many cities have several. Washington, DC, has ten, and more are being formed all the time. This has all come about since 1980, and in my view, it's one of the most important things that has happened in the common law for years.

The Inns have avoided the dangers of elitism, as anyone who has attended their meetings will know. Certainly, they're a terrific network, but the only qualification for membership is a keen determination to learn. There was an immense demand for places at the outset and many people had to be turned away, but that demand led to

* www.innsofcourt.org

the founding of new Inns. If things carry on at the present rate of expansion, no one who really wants to be a member will be disappointed.

I personally look forward to the time when there's an Inn for every 200 or so attorneys, and when Inn membership is the norm for every lawyer. A professional "home" is something the American attorney has long had to do without, and many have envied the British the collegiality of their Inns of Court. As a member of both an old and a new Inn, I can vouch for this: although there are no ancient rafters and no black gowns, America has incorporated all that was, and is, best about the original Inns of Court. The companionship is wonderful, the sense of actually doing something about the problems facing the profession is very strong, and the teaching provided is invaluable.

This book on advocacy, and the seminar on which it is based, is one lawyer's contribution. Advice and encouragement came to me from many sources. I am particularly grateful to Judge William B. Enright and to David Monahan of Gray, Cary, Ames & Frye, both of San Diego, who were the first to read and critique the script of the seminar. My thanks also go to Professor Sherman L. Cohn of Georgetown Law Center, the President of the American Inns of Court Foundation, to Judge James N. Barr, and to Vern Schooley, both of Orange County, to Ralph L. Dewsnup of Salt Lake City, and to Michael W. Coffield of Chicago, all of whom recognized the need for this kind of teaching and were especially instrumental in supporting it. I also want to thank Chug Roberts, of West Publishing Co., whose enthusiastic and sensitive editing of the script of the seminar helped to produce this book. Lastly, my warmest gratitude to Judy Prevatte and Susan Walton, my secretaries, for all their cheerful and untiring assistance, and to Denise Couch for her magical help with the word processing.

By serendipity rather than design, these Common Sense Rules, when we counted them up, numbered exactly one hundred. But I certainly don't want to suggest that all Common Sense Rules of Advocacy have been tracked down and included in this book. There are bound to be others, rules that I haven't personally come across, or haven't formulated. And that is where you, the reader can help. If a new rule occurs to you and you are willing to share it, please get in touch and tell me about it. I can be contacted through my [Publisher, Chug Roberts, at TheCapitol.Net, PO Box 25706, Alexandria, VA 22313-5706; www.TheCapitol.Net; 202-678-1600], and I very much look forward to seeing this collection added to.

Keith Evans
San Diego, California
December, 1993

About the Author

Keith Evans is a retired member of the Bars of both England and California, a Scholar of the Middle Temple Inn of Court in London, a member of Gray's Inn and a former Honorary Master of San Diego's Louis M. Welsh American Inn of Court.

He studied law at Cambridge and started trial practice as an English Barrister in 1963. From 1975 until 1996 he was an active member of the California Bar.

He has handled several hundred jury trials and has practiced in state and federal courts as well as, in England, every court from the Old Bailey to the House of Lords.

He was forced to retire (while, as he puts it, on a winning run) after suffering a stroke in 1998.

The holder of an Outstanding Trial Lawyer award from the San Diego Trial Lawyer's Association, he is also a distinguished teacher of trial advocacy. His book on the subject is the standard text in England and in many parts of the British Commonwealth.

He has been a visiting professor at an American university law school and has been on the faculty of NITA, and he still teaches a highly acclaimed full-day CLE seminar on trial advocacy.

He practiced with several firms in the United States, including Gray, Cary in San Diego and the aviation litigation firm of Speiser, Krause & Cook in New York City and Washington, DC.

Summary Table of Contents

CONTENTS

Table of Contents

CHAPTER ONE

Introduction

Skillful advocacy is a rare commodity. Although every generation produces its small handful of great advocates and a variable crop of really competent ones, the bulk of attorneys appearing in our courts never perform as they could—and should.

It's been the same for centuries, all over the English-speaking world. It's because we don't operate a system that guarantees a trial lawyer will really know what he or she is doing before handling a trial. Qualify as an attorney and you immediately have the right to screw up somebody's case in court. We lawyers have been left with a huge field in which to demonstrate our incompetence.

Certainly, there is advocacy training available. The invitations we get to attend this seminar or that three-day program are incessant. And some of them are superlative: they deliver what they promise. But despite mandatory continuing legal education there is still no system in place that requires you to show that you know what you are doing *before* you go into court.

Looked at from the point of view of the young advocate, we see the other, equally truthful, side of the coin. We are scared stiff of our first trials—always were. Our biggest fears are, one, that we are going to make fools of ourselves and, two, that we'll meet something we've never met before and just not know what to do.

"Tell me, Mr. Evans," says the judge, interrupting my opening, "is this a *Smith-v-Manchester* kind of case?"

"*Smith-v-Manchester*?" I ask myself. "*What* is a *Smith-v-Manchester* kind of case?"

It can be terrifying, and it usually takes years of practice to build one's confidence as an advocate. During those years—if we ever *get* the chance of trial work—most of us learn mainly by trial and error. And that, when you think about it, means the *client's* trial and the *lawyer's* error.

One day, perhaps, things will be different. The time may come when we look back and wonder how we could have allowed our courts of law, *the* most important protectors of our freedoms and of our empowerment, to be populated with under-trained advocates. And how we could have permitted to continue, all these centuries, the despairing disbelief of the client who suddenly realizes his lawyer is hopeless.

Trial advocacy is a skill that can be *taught*. If the teacher is competent and if the student has the right frame of mind, and is willing to devote not more than ten minutes a day to *thinking* about advocacy, then *anyone* capable of passing the bar is also capable of becoming an excellent trial lawyer. It is not a mystery: it is a skill.

Skills can be acquired.

This book makes a promise. If you devote three minutes a day to reading something in it, then another seven minutes thinking about what you have read, in two months you will already be better than 85 percent of the competition. If you really interest yourself in advocacy and take it seriously, you'll almost certainly find yourself among the 10 percent best trial lawyers in the country. After that, native genius takes over and it's up to you.

By the time you come to the end of this book—and it's easy reading because it's based upon the text of a live, one-day seminar—you ought to find yourself feeling that good advocacy is mostly a matter of common sense. The trouble is that we lawyers often leave common sense behind when we go into court. As a result we often seem boring, pompous, and devious, and we make the most unnecessary mistakes again and again. We are so preoccupied with the complexities and the pressures of our position we forget all the common sense simplicities. It's a barrier peculiar to the profession. Unless warned, almost all of us start out this way.

This book is about the common sense of advocacy. It's organized into a series of rules, most of which should seem obvious when you've seen them, but not necessarily so obvious that you knew about them in advance. The rules are illustrated clearly enough to demonstrate how they work, but the book doesn't contain more illustration than necessary. It is not a compendium of war stories, mine or anybody else's.

Get to know what these basic rules are, think about them and keep thinking about them, and you will avoid those miserable pitfalls that I fell into, along with most of my contemporaries.

If you are ready, let's get started.

CHAPTER TWO

The Dimensions of Advocacy

We live in a three-dimensional world: up and down, sideways, and to and fro. This is the hollow box in which human existence takes place. There are three fundamental truths which are so important to the advocate you can think of them as being the equivalent of the dimensions in which we live. All advocacy takes place in the context of these three truths. This is what they are.

First Dimension
In the Common-Law Countries, a Trial Is Not an Exercise Designed to Discover the Truth

The factfinding tribunal—whether judge alone or jury—is not being asked to discover the truth about anything. Focus on just a handful of things you already know very well:

- The rules of evidence are mainly designed to exclude. The exclusionary rules often operate to prevent the evidence actually presented from showing the truth of the matter at all.
- The jury rarely asks questions and, if it does, it is often told it can't have the answer.
- Personal knowledge of the dispute before the court can disqualify not only jurors but judges as well.
- Too much exposure of the jury panel to press and television reporting is ground for shifting venue.
- The judge is not an investigator.
- The jury is not a committee of inquiry.

We could go on but we don't need to. Although it is hardly ever thought about and although it causes raised eyebrows even among lawyers, the shocking fact remains: we are *not* principally concerned with getting at the truth in the courtrooms of the English-speaking peoples. What we are doing as advocates is trying to get the factfinder to arrive at an *opinion*, an opinion in our client's favor. We are asking: "On the admissible evidence presented in this trial—evidence which the judge has not told you to disregard—is it your *opinion* that this side succeeds or the other side?"

This doesn't mean you have a license to be dishonest. Anything but. And we'll come to honesty and advocacy quite soon. You most certainly can't lie and you have to be desperately careful about concealing anything. But, it's worth repeating, our objective at trial is *not* the ultimate truth, but an opinion in our client's favor.

Remember this: by the time you get to trial, discovery is over. The search for the truth is finished and you are no longer conducting an inquiry. Rather, *you are putting on a presentation designed to persuade*. By realizing this, your whole attitude toward trial should change slightly. If you thought about trial as a contest or a duel, start thinking about trial now as a tightly controlled presentation.

Second Dimension

This second dimension is as different from the first as up and down is different from to and fro. It is this:

Human Beings Are Far More Video than Audio

The way we collect most of our information is through our eyesight. Consider the use we make of our senses. In today's world, touch is used mainly for enjoyment: we get a lot of information from handling things, but touch is a subsidiary sense. Smell is much the same for us humans, and so is taste: as devices by which we collect information, touch, smell, and taste take a backseat to sight and hearing. And when you compare sight and hearing, you realize that the modern human being's principal means of fact gathering, of learning, and of understanding, is eyesight.

We don't have a phrase *hearing is believing.* We are used to television, video, cinema, newsprint, books. Intent listening is something we do with surprising rarity. Drive along with an education tape in your player, a tape designed to bring you up to date on some legal topic. How many times have you found your mind wandering, realizing that for several minutes you just haven't heard a thing? You nod off in your listening far more readily and easily than in your seeing.

What most lawyers ask the factfinders to do in court is to use their *second-best device* for gathering understanding. And the factfinders do it: on the whole they do it well. But since we don't tie blindfolds on them, they don't switch off their *best* information-gathering device. It is operating *all the time* while we are appealing to their second-best device.

This obvious truth, this second dimension of reality we are operating in, has to be remembered at *all times.* People who have studied the psychology of communications have some terrifying statistics for us lawyers. Examples:

- 60 percent of a message is conveyed by body language and visual appearance generally.
- 30 percent of a message is conveyed by tone of voice.
- Only 10 percent of a message comes through the words used.

- Only 10 percent of what people hear gets remembered. If, on the other hand, they *see* something connected with what they are hearing, *as they are hearing it*, they remember 50 percent.

They didn't tell me these things in law school. I wasn't given this information during my apprenticeship. Lawyers tend not to know these statistics, just as they don't seem to realize that they are operating virtually all the time in the Video Dimension.

Yet from the moment you enter the courthouse, the chances are you are going to be seen by one or more jurors. When you are in the courtroom itself, you are under the scrutiny of the jury almost full time. This means you are conveying visual messages to the jurors the whole day through. You can't help it.

We all have body language. Without realizing what we are signaling, we are in fact signaling something all the time. Since we can't help it, we simply must know what we are conveying. Appearances count more in the courtroom than most lawyers are prepared to admit or think about. But we are public performers. No less than the actor, the fashion model, and the politician, we are making a visual impression all the time and we must know what that impression is.

Although we may be embarrassed by the idea and perhaps a little shy, we ought to stand regularly in front of a mirror, talking and moving and gesturing, simply to get to know ourselves and to *stay* knowing ourselves. Try it tonight. See how long you have to look at the most familiar face in the world before a complete stranger looks back at you. It takes a little less than two minutes with most people.

The adult human hardly ever gets a completely new and objective view of himself or herself, but we advocates have a duty to stay in touch with ourselves and know how we are coming across, visually, to the rest of the world. The video recorder is a wonderful tool for self-awareness. Seeing yourself on video can be intimidating, but it will show you things you just hadn't been aware of: how you move your head, what you do with your mouth, your nose, your eyebrows, and, particularly, your eyes. It will show you how you move your hands, your arms, and your body generally. The lines on your forehead and around your nose are especially important. This is because they are the principal components of the frown and the sneer and can easily make you look anxious, or, far worse, disdainful. You can't know how your body is communicating without making a study of yourself.

As soon as you admit to yourself that yes, this Video Dimension is real, some practical rules are staring at you. The more you think about it, the more you'll see, but the most obvious rules are the following:

Rule 1
You Must Dress Appropriately

It has been said by one judge that in her court the lawyer who wears polyester has the burden of proof. Jurors have surprisingly high expectations of trial lawyers, and dress is important. The colors you wear, and that your client and witnesses wear, are much more significant than most of us ever pause to think about. If you've never encountered any of the studies that have been done on the impact of color, you should consider attending a seminar by an expert in the field. Until you have seen it physically demonstrated, you are unlikely to appreciate what an astonishing effect appropriate and inappropriate color can have on the impression made by the wearer.

It can even raise ethical questions. Since dressing in the "right" colors can make a person seem healthier and altogether more vital, just as dressing in the "wrong" colors can have the quite opposite effect, what should you do with a client who is constantly in pain but trying to be brave about it? Should she dress so as to look as healthy as possible, or should her colors be chosen so as to make her seem as unhealthy as she is? You'll find a fuller explanation of color considerations in Appendix 1, Why Color is Critical.

Rule 2
Don't Be Seen to Be in Too Friendly a Relationship with Your Opponent

This is particularly important in courts where you know your opponents well. Even if you are the greatest of friends outside the courtroom, it is your duty when in the courthouse to conceal this. Plain courtesy is enough. Be pleasant but not friendly. The reason for this ought to be clear: if a juror or jurors should happen to see you, outside court or on your way to the courthouse, in an obviously friendly encounter with your opponent, and then see you, in court, in an adversarial situation with the same person, they are going to wonder about your sincerity. Is your advocacy some sort of act in court, some kind of game? You don't want to give your jurors *any* reason not to trust you.

Rule 3

Don't Smile, Laugh, or Joke without Including the Jury in

Nothing is so off-putting as seeing laughter and joking in front of you without knowing what is going on and being able to share in the fun.

Rule 4

Appear at All Times to Be Absolutely Sincere

If you fail in this even one time, you undermine your chances for the whole of the rest of the case.

Rule 5

Never Convey Any Visual Signal You Do Not Intend to Convey

This means you must never seem *surprised* unless you intend to, you must never seem *troubled* unless you intend to, and you must never seem to be *expending effort* unless you intend to. This is particularly important when you are cross-examining. We'll return to variations on this rule when we come to Chapter 8.

Let me, incidentally, give you an encouraging hint. When you go to a new court or to take a deposition in new company, the only person who knows about your inexperience, nervousness, and limitations is you yourself. To the rest of the world you may be a lawyer of vast experience and lethal talent. Don't throw away the advantage of their not knowing.

The rules discussed so far all arise naturally out of the need to guard against *dangers* of the Video Dimension. But it can be taken advantage of as well. Think how. It can be summarized in one obvious practical rule:

Rule 6
Ensure that Your Factfinder Always Has Something to Look at

Since they are going to be using their eyes, provide them with a focus. Some lawyers are superlative at this. What do they do?

They:

Rule 7
Use All Kinds of Visual Aids

Most courts have a board on the wall with a giant pad of paper on it. It's known as butcher paper. If your courts don't have such a pad, take one with you, along with an easel to prop it on. Use the pad. Print on it with thick markers. Do sums. Draw pictures. Write things up so that you can strike them out. Be creative. And another hint here: take along an overlay of transparent plastic. When you have finished whatever it is you are doing and go to sit down, your opponent, if she is imaginative, may grab a marker and start drawing or writing all over your product. There's nothing in the rules to prevent it and I've seen it done. If you use a transparent overlay and she still messes up your diagram, list, or whatever, you'll be able to complain with justification and she'll have alienated the factfinder.

Use blow-ups and overhead projectors. If you have the clause in the contract you say was breached in three-inch-high letters, right in front of the jury on a board three feet by four feet, they will look at it and keep looking at it. If you put up a transparency of a question and answer from a deposition so that it is there on a cinema screen in front of the factfinder while you cross-examine, the impact is enormous. Use a projector for photographic slides, flicking from one to the next as you explain them. People *listen* far more intently if they have something to look at connected with what they are hearing and so remember, according to the statistics, up to five times as much. And if you can get a video into court, get one. If you can get a model of some sort, get one of those, too, particularly models that come apart. They appeal to the child in us as well as to the adult and focus attention quite wonderfully. Always give them something to look at.

Equally important:

Rule 8

Maintain Eye Contact with the Factfinder

Don't overdo it. The direct stare is usually seen as a threat in the animal kingdom and the human being is no exception. The regular glance is enough, resting on your factfinder's eyes long enough not to seem shifty, and briefly enough not to seem threatening or intrusive. You not only stay in touch this way: you usually get a lot of feedback, feedback from which you can gauge how you are doing.

Enough then about the Video Dimension. When you've seen how important it is, you can start to work out for yourself how to guard against it and take advantage of it. Be creative.

The third dimension is as different from the first two as they were from each other. Come now to the next absolutely fundamental truth.

Third Dimension
People Don't Like Lawyers!

We have been near the bottom of the popularity polls for centuries, keeping company with executioners, horse-traders, and debt-collectors. What's the latest funny remark about us? "What do you say about 500 attorneys at the bottom of the ocean?—A good start!" Come back to Fourteenth Century England, at the time of the Peasants' Revolt. The first place the mob made for was the Inns of Court. They torched them. A contemporary account:

"It was marvelous to see how the most aged and infirm of them scrambled off with the agility of rats or evil spirits!"

Or how about the Eighteenth Century? Dr. Samuel Johnson:

"I don't care to speak ill of anyone behind his back, but I do believe that gentleman is an attorney."

Or the Nineteenth Century—Sir John Simon:

"The public see the lawyer as an unprincipled wretch who is constantly engaged in the distortion of the truth by methods entirely discreditable and for rewards grossly exaggerated. He is expected to be a hypocrite."

There are so many in the Twentieth Century, take just one. Will Rogers, cowboy, filmstar, wit, Mayor of Beverly Hills, insightful commentator on American life:

"It's a man's lack of conscience enables him to be a lawyer."

People mistrust us, and, sad to say, there are enough bad apples in the barrel of the legal profession to justify such mistrust. People are afraid of us. In many ways they *despise* us. "Ignorance of the law doesn't prevent the losing attorney from collecting his fee."

So what practical rules arise out of this sorry but quite fundamental truth? How do we work against this awesome prejudice? Let me give you just three.

Rule 9
Stick Rigorously to the Truth

There actually is a way in which every case can be conducted with absolutely total honesty. No lawyer ever needs to be a liar. There is no need at all for a trial lawyer to be two-faced. Search for the way in which you can present your case in *total sincerity*. Quite apart from anything else, the composite mind that a jury becomes has an incredible nose for insincerity. If you don't believe what you are asking them to believe, then make no mistake about it: *they will know*.

Too many lawyers don't realize this. And it's lawyers like them who have earned us the public image we all suffer from. If you can't find a way of doing a case with utmost sincerity, then settle or plea-bargain out, or get someone else to do it. But it doesn't have to come to that. There is a sincere way of conducting every case. Find it.

Imagine, for example, a criminal case. You are defending someone in the teeth of really tough evidence. His story just isn't credible. You dare not put him on the stand. What do you do? You have to have recourse to the burden of proof and, if it applies, to due process. You hammer home the importance of due process, the even greater importance that no one can be convicted unless the offense is proved beyond a reasonable doubt. You tell them what reasonable doubt is all about; you tell the jury that unless they have been corralled by the prosecutor's evidence, unless they have been pushed into a corner by it so that they are left with no sensible choice in the matter, then they *must* come in with a not guilty verdict. Paint the picture for them of what a messy failure a miscarriage of justice is. Tell them about the way it has happened in the past. Put the fear of God in them over what would happen to America if we didn't take the burden of proof as seriously as we do. If your client gets convicted after that, he's almost certainly guilty. There is always a totally honest way of presenting a case. Find it and do it that way.

Rule 10
Don't Appear to Be Manipulative

We all know when we are being manipulated. If it's your five-year-old daughter doing it, it can be charming. In most other situations it's offensive. If you make the jury feel that you are manipulating them, they'll feel that you are living down to their expectations and they'll mistrust you for it. Take care, too, not to come across as a manipulator of witnesses.

Rule 11
Don't Sound like a Lawyer

This isn't easy. We spent all those years in law school learning a whole new vocabulary as well as a whole new way of thinking. It's *our* vocabulary: we like it: it's useful.

"Sergeant Sullivan," said the President of the Court of Appeal, "Hasn't your client ever heard of *in pari delicto portior est conditio defendentis*?"

"My Lord," replied the great Irish advocate, "In the hills and dales of Killarney where my client plies his trade as a shepherd, they talk of little else!"

Don't use it! Don't use *any* lawyer's language at all. Aim to get through the whole case, start to finish, without using the word "testimony" once.

People don't control motor vehicles, they drive cars.

They don't enter into contractual arrangements, they make deals.

They don't testify, they tell us.

Examine your language from this day on. Strip out *anything* that sounds lawyerish. Find some other way of saying what you want to say so that no one would guess you have a J.D., let alone that you were an attorney. Work hard at this. The rule is absolutely clear: *do not sound like a lawyer.*

Those, then, are the three fundamental truths, the three dimensions in the context of which all trial advocacy takes place. But in real life there is an extra, a fourth, dimension, and it is very much there in court as well.

Fourth Dimension
Time Is Valuable

Time. Your time. My time. It's expensive stuff. Some of you, perhaps most of you, measure your profitability by time. Billable hours mean time. Time to the lawyer can be enemy or paymaster. Time is a demanding mistress, a jealous lover, a jailer, a slave driver.

It can also be elastic. Compare ten minutes making love with ten minutes having a root canal fixed. And think of how long-drawn-out six hours in a jury box listening to an incompetent, wasteful attorney can be. Most jurors have better things to do with their time. We don't usually pay them enough to park their car, and they are giving their time as a public duty. They have to rush around outside court hours getting everything done just so they can sit there and listen to you, *you*, hour after hour, day after day, perhaps even week after week.

And what about the judge? Do you know how much she has waiting to be done, on the other side of the corridor? Do you know how much paper he has to look at just to stay abreast of the workload?

This is the fourth dimension in which you operate as a trial lawyer, and if you forget it, if you forget it for one moment of your factfinder's precious time, look out! If you *ever* give them cause to feel that you are wasting their time, they will resent you for it, and if you get your factfinder feeling resentful about you, you are a good halfway to losing your case. This is far, far more important than most lawyers realize.

It's worse than that. It's not just that the inexperienced attorney hasn't grasped the problems of the Fourth Dimension. This is an opposite pressure that works on us and we usually give way before it. It's a two-pronged thing.

First prong: You've got a client. The client is almost certainly in court, listening intently to everything. You feel this huge obligation to make sure she feels she is getting her money's worth. You have this strong conviction that you ought to be giving her so many questions in cross-examination, so many square feet of transcript. If you don't do this, isn't she going to feel that you didn't do your best for her, that you sold her short, that you let her down?

Sure. She may indeed. And she would be as wrong as you were. This is something you must talk to her about in advance. This is part of the *private advocacy* that goes on between attorney and client. You've got to explain it, make her understand the Fourth Dimension, make her appreciate that brevity is your secret weapon. When she sees the quality of attention you are getting from your factfinder, she'll stop worrying about it, but, yes, you do have a duty to explain all this to your client in advance.

Second prong: The other kind of pressure that will push you into wasting time is your own insecurity. You'll be convinced that you didn't make yourself clear enough, didn't say it forcefully enough, didn't get your point across adequately. And you will repeat yourself. It's so understandable, this fear, this anxiety. We've all suffered from it and know the pressure.

Don't yield to it.

Rule 12
Don't Repeat Yourself

Take your courage in both hands, say it once as clearly as you can and *don't say it twice*. The exceptions to this are very few and we'll come to them later—in Chapter 5, when we consider *Rule 54*.

Now, one last point before we move on. Can you take *advantage* of the Dimension of Time? We saw that the Video Dimension had advantages as well as dangers, and we thought through how to tap in to those advantages. Can we do the same with time? Certainly we can, and it's easy.

All you have to do is remember, now and again, to drop in a phrase to remind everybody that time is something you are aware of.

"I want to deal with this as briefly as I can, Mr. Witness."

"Well, I don't want to take up any more time on that point. Let's move on."

"Very well, let me move quickly to something else. I want to ask you about . . . ."

You don't have to use these particular phrases. Anything along these lines will do. Just make sure that you get across to your judge or judge and jury, every day, preferably twice a day, that you know the importance of their time. Their time. They'll appreciate it.

The Mandatory Rules of Advocacy

Before we get down to looking at the practical rules that apply to all advocacy, let's spend a little while on a small handful of rules that should be thought of as mandatory. These rules *must* be observed. If you break them you'll show yourself to be unprofessional. Some of these mandatory rules are so important that breaking them can lead to a retrial or even to a lost case. Since they are so few there is no excuse for not knowing them. What are they?

Rule 13
Mandatory Rule Number One: In Your Opening Statement, Avoid All Argument and Stick Strictly to Facts

This mandatory rule means just what it says. It is at the other end of the trial, in your closing argument, that you are allowed to argue, to invite the factfinder to draw inferences, to quote Mark Twain. In your opening statement, the only thing you are permitted to do is tell your factfinder what you expect your evidence to prove. And bear this in mind: since you'll only be allowed to introduce evidence that is relevant, this means you can only tell your factfinder about relevant matters, matters that you are convinced you will be allowed to prove. Beware of talking about anything in the opening that you are later prevented from proving: it can and sometimes does lead to a mistrial.

If, in order to make the facts comprehensible to the jury, it is essential to explain something about the law and about the way the law and the evidence are going to fit together, then you are permitted to do this as well. But make sure that your judge and your opponent know about this in advance. Clear it with them in the pre-trial conference. Do not just stand up and launch into it—otherwise you'll attract an objection and that objection will be sustained. And having objections sustained against you in your opening statement is *not* a good way to start.

Does being forced to stick to the simple facts—no argument, no quotes from Mark Twain—sound rather limiting? It's not. Illustration:

> "Ladies and gentlemen, let me tell you what I expect the evidence to prove in this case that you've sworn to try. It actually *was* a dark and stormy evening. Winter was coming on and the road through the mountains was wet and slippery. Squalls were bringing sudden heavy showers of rain. Driving along that road in a little blue car were Jane and Richard Roe. They were two weeks married. Jane was a kindergarten teacher. Richard had just finished his internship as a pediatrics doctor. They were both keen tennis players. Jane was a champion gymnast. Because of the intermittent rain and the condition of the road, they were going carefully, rarely traveling faster than 40 m.p.h. It was Richard who was at the wheel . . . ."

Do you want to know what happened next? Can you feel the mounting sense of doom? Apart from the color of the car not a word of this is irrelevant. There is *no* argument. It's nothing but fact.

We'll talk about what we are doing here when we come to the general practical rules, but before turning to the next of the mandatory rules, let me point out one thing. You notice that that little story wasn't constantly interrupted by the phrase, "The evidence will show." We said, once, at the very beginning, "Let me tell you what I expect the evidence to prove . . ." and then got straight into the story. Don't pepper your openings with "The evidence will show"—it makes you sound like a beginner or extremely unimaginative.

Rule 14
Mandatory Rule Number Two: Be Sure, in Your Opening Statement, to State Enough Facts to Justify the Verdict You Are Asking for

If you fail to observe this rule, then in some jurisdictions your opponent is entitled, there and then, to a directed verdict against you. It doesn't matter that the testimony, if and when it came out, would plug the gaps in what you said. It is your duty to state enough facts in your opening so that, if everything turns out as you want it to, you will be clearly entitled to the verdict you are asking for.

Take particular care when you are asking for more than one verdict—as in civil cases where there are different causes of action, and as in criminal cases where there are several counts on the indictment. Your opening statement must contain enough facts to justify *all* the verdicts you are asking for. If you fail in this, you may find even at this early stage in the trial that some of your causes of action or some of your counts just get stricken.

This can happen to the advocate who doesn't know this mandatory rule. Imagine the difficulties he would have in trying to make the client understand. And if the client sued for malpractice, would there be any defense? This mandatory rule can be stated and explained in two short paragraphs, but if you ever forget to apply it, you could be in deep trouble.

Rule 15

Mandatory Rule Number Three:
The Advocate Must Not Express
His or Her Opinion in Court

Since this rule is broken all over the country every day the courts are sitting, it's important to understand the rule clearly. Let's consider some basic ideas. First, an attorney appearing at a trial is a licensed professional. You are there to represent only one side of the dispute—a kind of hired champion. Think of what the job involves. What are its limits? You are there to present and test the evidence as effectively as possible, to present and argue the relevant law when you deal with motions or objections, then to sum up the whole lot as attractively as you can. That's it. Your opinion about the merits of the case doesn't enter into that process, anywhere at all. Now come to the next consideration. These days most trial lawyers stick to one kind of job. They are plaintiffs' attorneys, or defense attorneys, prosecutors, or defenders. This is the way the system tends to operate now. But it's a fairly recent development and it was not always so. For hundreds of years the advocate was a kind of roving freelancer, a professional who was ready to take either side of the dispute, depending who hired him first. This still happens today, out in the rural areas in America, and there is still a strict rule about it at the English Bar.

Since a lot of American trial practice has its roots in England, I think it's worth taking a moment to tell about this rather surprising English rule. It says this: if you are offered a case that is within your field of expertise, then, if the client is willing to pay what you usually charge and your calendar shows you are free to take the case—you don't have any choice in the matter. You *must* accept it. If you turn it down you can be disciplined, even disbarred! It's called "the cab-rank rule," and it came into existence in the first place to avoid unpopular defendants finding themselves at a trial with no one to represent them. It doesn't matter what you think of the case. It's your duty to take it and do your best for your client. It's absolutely irrelevant whether you think you are trying a winner or a loser.

Because of this rule, which everybody knows about in England, no one in court is ever going to embarrass you by asking what you actually think about the merits of your case; and although the cab-rank rule hasn't traveled the Atlantic, the protection it provides to the advocate *has* come to America. Some years ago, a federal judge was trying a difficult patent dispute without a jury. Counsel on both sides were nationally recognized experts in their field. The judge was having a devil of a time grappling with the problem, and at one stage, he threw down his pen in despair, and looked at the lawyer addressing him. "Oh, Mr. S_____," he said, "how I wish I could ask you what you really think about this case!" But he couldn't. Counsel is there to urge one side of the dispute. You are *not* allowed to express an opinion.

Another short illustration. The American revolutionary, Tom Paine, was put on trial in England on a political charge. He was defended by the leading barrister of the day, Thomas Erskine. The trial was about the liberty of the individual, and, although it isn't much remembered today, there was actually a huge amount of support in England for the American colonists. At one point Erskine, in a towering passion, said to the judge, "And now, My Lord, I will lay aside the role of advocate and address you as a man!" Lord Campbell, the judge trying the case, broke in on him at once. "You will do nothing of the sort!" he said. "The only right and license you have to appear in this court is as an advocate!" And the judge was absolutely right.

But the rule is broken all the time. "It is our opinion, ladies and gentlemen, that when you have heard the evidence, you'll have no difficulty in returning a verdict for the plaintiff." "I think, ladies and gentlemen, you will find the testimony of Mr. Fagin credible and satisfactory." "We feel that you'll be left in no doubt," etc.

What's so bad about all this? Surely it shows you are sincere? It may do so, but it's none of your business to tell the factfinder what you think. There is a real risk the jury will feel you are trespassing on their ground; but the real harm of expressing your opinion in court lies in the effect it has on the judge. Break this rule and it marks you off as unprofessional. It is the clearest signal that you have never heard of the rule, that you don't know your job properly. It makes the judge suspicious of you, makes her wonder what else you are going to do wrong, how much you can't be trusted. And if she feels this, you can be sure she'll be more ready to rule against you when the other side objects to something. You have tipped the balance of the judge's inclination in your opponent's favor.

So how do you cope? How do you manage to sound sincere without breaching this rule and branding yourself as unprofessional? It's very easy. You just avoid using the words, "I think" or "I believe" or "It's my opinion," when you are talking about anything to do with the merits of the case. Instead of saying, "I believe you will be convinced that . . . ," you say, "I trust that, when you have heard what the witnesses have to tell you, you will be convinced that . . . ." Instead of "we feel," you say, "we hope." You say it in a low, throwaway tone of voice, emphasizing the meat of the sentence that follows. You lose nothing at all in sincerity and impact, but you send a signal straight to your judge that *you* are an advocate who knows the No Opinion rule. And getting that message to your judge, that you know what you are doing, and getting it across as early as possible, is vital.

Rule 16

Mandatory Rule Number Four: As an Advocate, Never Give or Appear to Give Evidence Yourself

This rule should be obvious, but since I've often seen it broken, let me spell it out. Here is an illustration of the kind of thing I mean. I had a pupil, once, at the English Bar. He happened to get brought in to a case I was trying. I represented one defendant: he represented the other. It was a criminal matter in front of a jury. He did it beautifully. He cross-examined skillfully although he was trembling like a leaf. He argued points of admissibility like an expert. I was proud of him and I was looking forward to see how he'd do in his final summation. He did that beautifully too, but all of a sudden I heard him say: "And, do you know, members of the jury, I was talking to my client over the lunch hour and he told me . . . !" Up went the judge's eyebrows. Up jumped our opponent, spluttering an objection. I grabbed my pupil's gown and hissed in his ear. He turned quickly to something else, but later, when the jury had gone out he came to me, really bewildered. "What did I do wrong?" I explained. "You never told me that before," he said reproachfully. And I realized that what was obvious to me may not be obvious to everyone else. *Testimony comes from the witness stand, never from the attorney.* That trial, incidentally, had a nice ending for my pupil. His client was acquitted and mine was found guilty.

Rule 17

Mandatory Rule Number Five: Never Refer to the Criminal Record of an Accused Person or to Any Offers of Settlement

If you fail to observe this mandatory rule you'll almost certainly have a mistrial on your hands. In the rarest, the very rarest, of circumstances, there may be exceptions to the rule. In a cutthroat criminal defense between several accused being tried together, it may be permissible for one to refer to the criminal record of another. In very rare cases the prosecutor may be entitled to prove the accused's previous convictions. But these rare exceptions involve the law of evidence and criminal procedure, and no advocate worth the name would break this rule without undertaking the most careful research *and* getting the prior approval of the judge.

Likewise, it is conceivable that a case might occur when an offer of settlement became relevant to the trial itself. Again, it would be a matter of scrupulously careful research *and* prior approval from the judge before you breathe a word about it in court.

I can't guarantee to refer you to all the "never refers" in the different jurisdictions. As long as you know the rule and make a point of checking locally you won't make any ghastly mistakes.

Rule 18

Mandatory Rule Number Six: Never Put Words into the Mouth of Your Own Witness

Another way of stating this mandatory rule is: "Don't ask any leading questions of your witnesses," but if you think of it as *not putting words into their mouths* you sidestep the confusion that can sometimes arise over what is or what is not a leading question.

What exactly is a leading question? It's a question that contains its own answer. A leading question can be answered with a "Yes" or "No," with a nod or a shake of the head. Illustrations:

> *You are now 27 years old?*—Yes.
> *You were born in Boston, Massachusetts?*—Yes.
> *You fought at Lexington, is that right?*—Yes.
> *And you were wounded there?*—Yes.

Every question here contains its own answer. All the witness has to do is agree.

If we change those questions so as to eliminate the answers they contain, they become:

> *How old are you?*—Twenty seven.
> *Where were you born?*—Boston, Massachusetts.
> *Did you play any part at Lexington?*—I was in the fighting.
> *How did you fare, personally?*—I was wounded.

Just because a question can be answered with a nod or a shake of the head, it doesn't follow that it's leading. But the other way around the rule is firm. A leading question can always be answered by a grunt, a nod, a shake of the head, a "Yes" or "No." A leading question always gives the witness the chance of adopting or rejecting the information it already contains.

So what is so bad about leading questions? Why do the rules say you can't use them on your own witnesses? Because with leading questions *the testimony is coming not from the witness but from the advocate*. Leading questions offend against Mandatory Rule Number Four—no evidence from the advocate—but leading questions are offensive for two other very good reasons:

First: If the evidence comes from you and is merely adopted by your witness, how can the factfinder assess the witness's credibility? If all they hear is a series of yes or no answers they have nothing to go on. Your witness might have been someone you hired from a temp agency just to come to court to say "Yes" or "No" at appropriate places.

Second: If *you* give the testimony by putting words into your witness's mouth, you are ruining the value of that testimony. You are diluting the effect of your witness's testimony to the point where it may be virtually useless. Jurors interviewed at the end of trials have been asked about this and they are surprisingly clear in what they say. They easily recognize that testimony obtained by leading questions is pretty worthless. It is obvious to them the witness was simply saying what the lawyer wanted her to say. And this reminds them, subconsciously—and sometimes consciously—of the Third

Dimension: People Don't Like Lawyers. People don't trust us. If you let the jury feel your witness is only saying what you want her to say, you not only diminish the value of her testimony, you also kindle the resentment of the jury. You lose both ways. So it's not only a mandatory rule that you don't put words into your own witness's mouth: it's an obvious practical rule of advocacy as well. Although there are exceptions to this mandatory rule (discussed in *Rules 61–65* that appear in Chapter 7) and although there are many instances where you *can* use leading questions on your own witnesses, be aware of the dangers. Even when you are allowed to, use leading questions with the utmost care.

Rule 19

Mandatory Rule Number Seven: In Your Closing Argument, Speak Only of Things that Have Been Touched Upon in the Evidence

How strictly must this mandatory rule be observed? Aren't there any generalities I can talk about so as to spice up my closing remarks? If, in an environmental case, I want to talk about the ecological dangers that the planet is facing, or, in a drug case, discuss the way the authorities seem to be losing in the war against the traffickers—can't I do this? Does it all have to be "touched on" during the evidence stage before I can refer to any generalities at all?

No, of course not. You can always talk about things that really are common knowledge. You can always refer to verses from the Bible, quotes from Shakespeare and Mark Twain. You don't have to prove by testimony where San Francisco is located. If, on the other hand, you needed to refer to the exact mileage between San Francisco and downtown Los Angeles, that's something you should have raised during the evidence phase. You could probably have got the judge to take judicial notice of the distance and avoid having to call a witness, but you cannot refer to details like that without some kind of proof. The dividing line is almost always obvious. If you know this mandatory rule it should cause you no difficulty. You can refer to historical events and characters, to characters out of TV soaps, and you can talk about anything that is common knowledge. But if you want to talk about anything that *might* have been proved, make sure that you *did* prove it before referring to it in your summation.

There is one other mandatory rule, the Foundation Rule, but this is much more conveniently discussed in Chapter 7, Direct Examination.

So much, then, for the mandatory rules. Now let's take a trip to the theater.

CHAPTER FOUR

Advocacy as Theater

Listen to the following fragment of conversation:

"What was your jury duty like?"
"Great! Better than watching television."

"But wasn't it boring?"
"Boring? You've got to be kidding! It was like being at the theater all the way through."

"But wasn't it difficult, coming to a decision?"
"Heck no. By the time we had to reach a verdict it was a foregone conclusion."

"Would you do it again?"
"You bet!"

A fictitious conversation? That is what your juror should be telling his friends after a trial *you* conducted. I'll break one of my own rules by repeating myself. You are a licensed professional. The court of law is theater. Your job is to make it professional theater.

You wouldn't want to be a trial lawyer if there wasn't something of an actor inside of you. You'd have gone for another job or another area of law practice. By aiming for the courtroom, you have chosen to go on the professional stage, just as surely as if you'd tried to make it in Hollywood or on Broadway.

Admit this to yourself. Sure, you like the status of being an attorney. You like the rewards and the prospects. But there's a part of you that's stage-struck. If there isn't a part of you that's stage-struck, be forewarned, because those of us who *are* are going to be your competition. You'll always be at a disadvantage. If you can't reach into yourself and find the actor, move over to transactional lawyering. You're probably better off drafting contracts and leases. You'll certainly be safer back in the office where you don't have to put yourself on the line every time you stand up and open your mouth— where you don't have to take your courage in both hands and risk screwing up in public every time you go to court.

Trial lawyering is the sharp end of the law. It's where the real action is. As an advocate you've got to know how to handle fright— fear that rarely goes away completely—and handle it so no one would ever guess. To be an advocate, you've got to be an actor and you've got to be a brave one.

This needs to be said and it needs to be faced. It's the basic, rock-bottom truth of what real trial lawyering is all about. It's the toughest kind of lawyering there is. It takes courage, it takes imagination, and it takes the ability to get up and keep going when your mouth goes dry and you want to burst into tears. And all without showing it—all, incidentally, without letting it break your heart and break your spirit.

If you are going to be a trial lawyer, here is your most important practical rule:

Rule 20

Commit to Being an Excellent Trial Lawyer. Don't Do Anything by Halves. If You Can't Dedicate Yourself to This, Move Over and Do Something Else.

If you do commit to it, if you honestly admit to yourself that this is what you want to do and do really well, then the chances are high you'll turn out to be really good. All the other practical rules of persuasion and advocacy are subordinate to this one.

You all have law degrees: you all passed the bar exam. By definition, you are some of the most intelligent people in society. If you really and truly dedicate yourself to becoming a first-class trial lawyer, it is almost certain you will succeed. If you don't do this, you will never be better than second-rate.

I don't need to say much more about this practical rule of wholehearted commitment. But I do have two comments on it, observations that may be less obvious to Americans than to those who have also practiced in other countries.

First is this fact. In the United States, you have a body of literature devoted to advocacy, and trial work generally, that is unique in the world of law. No other country even begins to compare. There are practice books here which spell out, line by line, how to pick a jury, how to cross-examine experts, how to frame objections. They give you the actual words to use. Then there are tapes for your car, videos for your home, all designed to show you how to do it. Don't, I beg of you, ignore this gold mine. Get into the habit of *browsing* in these books, sampling these tapes. Advocacy is far more than a trade, a craft, an art. It can become a way of life. Try to read just a little about advocacy every day. A paragraph is enough: just read *something* every day.

But beware of one thing. Don't become the slave to anything you read. You will find bad advice as well as good out there, and you'll learn as much from identifying the bad as you will from recognizing and adopting the good. If you take in and keep thinking about the principles discussed in this book, and bear them in mind as you go prospecting in this rich American gold mine, you'll know gold when you find it. Be critical. And remember that you don't need to imitate anybody. Set out to be your *own* kind of advocate. Don't be afraid of being individual. Read as widely as you can, but remember that you are uniquely you. Know the rules, understand why they are important, then do it your way.

And the *second* observation I want to make is this. If commitment to advocacy generally is vitally important, so is commitment to the individual case. And America is unique in this regard as well. The quality of preparation that goes into a case here is more intensive and more thorough than anywhere else in the world. Sure, there are exceptions, but as an overall American pattern, quality preparation is the rule.

The system here provides the opportunity for intensive preparation—far more so than is generally the case in England and the other common-law countries. In England, preparation can quite literally be a matter of reading your papers on the way to court, and there's a joke at the Old Bailey that defending barristers often don't know what the trial is about until they hear the prosecutor's opening. Like all jokes about lawyers, it's got some truth in it.

But in America, even if the case is assigned by the court, proper provision is almost always made for preparation. It will almost always be paid for. And because the opportunity for preparation is available to you, you have a duty to prepare intensively.

Prepare, and the rewards are guaranteed. You may not win your case, but you will impress your judge and jury from first to last. Nothing comes across more clearly. Obvious preparation, leading to a meticulous knowledge of the case, shines all the way through and *always* commands respect. Judges, asked what is the single most important thing about advocacy, say, again and again, "*preparation.*" It's the best investment of them all. There's no substitute for preparation, and lack of it is always found out.

If I am beginning to sound like a revivalist preacher, forgive me. But this is a passionately important message. All American liberties depend on the courts, and without a continuous supply of first-class advocates these astonishing liberties, which are so much taken for granted, are at risk. *You* are the generation whose skills are going to protect those liberties: this is *your* duty and privilege. It is *your* commitment.

Let me bring you back to the concept of the courtroom as theater.

Focus on the courtroom as theater and a handful of practical rules leap out at you. Let's look at what they are, let's examine some obvious buzzwords. What should theater be? What does it involve?

Entertainment. Drama. A good storyline. Profound attentiveness from the audience. Applause. A sense that the whole thing was worthwhile doing, worthwhile having gone to. Good theater is satisfying, moving, memorable. In good theater time never drags, the development of the play never flags, the audience never gets bored.

That's enough. There are enough ideas there. Let's take these out of the theater and across to the courtroom and see how our practical rules appear.

One thing is blindingly obvious, isn't it? In the law court your audience can't get up and leave.

They are in the truest sense captive. They aren't free to hiss and boo you off the stage. They are obliged to sit there, and this means that two things have to be borne in mind.

First: Although they are obliged to sit there, *they are not obliged to listen to you.*

Second: Since you have a captive audience, you owe it to them to make the trial as entertaining as you possibly can.

If you do make it entertaining, they'll listen to you. If you don't, the listening they do will be done out of a sense of duty: it won't be intent listening and it won't be sympathetic to you or your case.

So, as an obvious, practical rule of persuasion and advocacy, we have:

Rule 21
Entertain Them

—simple as that.

But hold on. It's an obvious practical rule. But you can't say, "Simple as that!" Stating the rule and putting it into operation—it's not the same thing. Is it?

To a large extent it is. I'll suggest a handful of easy-to-use *tools* for keeping your factfinder entertained, and I'll come to them in a moment. But first I want to emphasize something. Just as there is a magical element about the theater and acting, there's a magical element about the court and advocacy. Part of that magic is this: if you are simply aware of a rule and only *hope* you'll be able to put it into operation, you are unlikely to offend against it.

Take comfort from this because it's true. Simply by hoping to put the rules into effect you *will* put them into effect. You may not do it terribly well but you'll do it. Unless you are cursed with a total lack of imagination—and the chances of that are small—then merely by knowing what the rules are and thinking about them as you prepare for trial, you will almost certainly not break them. And this, as I said at the outset, will put you ahead of most of the competition.

But I said I had some easy-to-use tools for keeping your factfinder entertained. They are such basic, important techniques they can be thought of as practical rules in their own right.

First:

Rule 22

Tell Them a Story

Keep this idea in the forefront of your mind all the way through, from the beginning of your preparation to the end of the case. From your opening statement through to your final summation. No matter what you are doing, what stage of the case you are at, always keep asking yourself whether there is an element of storytelling in whatever you are giving them.

Why do I recommend this? Because no one can resist listening to a well-told story, even if they've heard it dozens of times before. This is how we human beings are. This is how we responded as children, listening with deep contentment to the same stories again and again. We never lose our capacity to respond. If we *feel* we are being told a story, if we sense that there is a story here, then our natural, instinctive response is to prick up our ears and let it flow into us. Look how you responded to those few lines about the couple in the car on the mountain road.

Some of what you do in court will literally be a story: your opening will be, certainly. But you should aim, with every witness you call, to turn the testimony into a story as well. Even your cross-examinations can have the flavor of story-telling if you do it right. *Think* story telling. If you do, you are likely to call into play your factfinder's natural impulse to listen.

Next, and very connected with the Story-Telling Rule:

Rule 23
Think Beginning, Middle, and End

If you do think beginning, middle, and end, you will automatically bring a shape to everything you do, whether it's an opening statement or a cross-examination. In particular, try to focus on how you intend to *end* whatever it is you are doing. This ensures, again almost automatically, that you always know where you are going. One of the rules we will come to when we deal with the examination of witnesses in Chapter 6 is the Always Know Your Objective Rule—*Rule 59*. If you make a habit of thinking beginning, middle, and end, with particular emphasis on end, you'll find that the Know Your Objective Rule almost takes care of itself.

The next tool for holding their attention and keeping them entertained is a rule you should have in mind all the way through the trial:

Rule 24
Always Aim to Maintain Your Continuity

When you have a pause, when, indeed, a pause is forced upon you because your mind goes blank—as happens to all of us—try to make even that pause part of the entertainment. It can be done, and it's not difficult. Let me share with you a technique I was taught years ago by an old trial lawyer.

We all know the fright of having our minds go blank on us. For the inexperienced advocate it's a real fear. But it needn't be. What the technique involves is this, and it works in three stages.

When you suddenly realize, with alarm, that your mind has gone blank—

Step one is to send a message to your stomach and command it to relax. This actually does control the flow of adrenaline, and, with it, the dry mouth and the raised heartbeat.

Step two is to pick up any piece of paper with writing, type, or printing on it, look intently at a blank margin, and silently count to three.

Step three is to glance up at your judge and say, "If Your Honor would give me a moment," then look *straight* back at your piece of paper.

You can have twenty seconds at that point, twenty seconds of total silence, if you need them, to gather your thoughts. Nobody is going to mind. Nobody is going to feel that you have interrupted the continuity or that you have had a breakdown in transmission. This is because *you have invested that pause with an apparent significance of its own*. You won't need twenty seconds. Your mind will clear much quicker than that, and on you go. The next practical rule for holding the factfinder's attention and keeping them entertained:

Rule 25
Keep It Simple

Consider just one sentence from George Washington's First Inaugural Address, April 30, 1789:

"All I dare hope is that if, in executing this task, I have been too much swayed by a grateful remembrance of former instances, or by an affectionate sensibility to this transcendent proof of the confidence of my fellow citizens, and have thence too little consulted my incapacity as well as disinclination for the weighty and untried cares before me, my error will be palliated by the motives which mislead me, and its consequences be judged by my country with some share of the partiality in which they originated."

Most people, today, are lost by halfway through the third line. If you are forced to read on, or listen on, the chances are you'll become as dazed as if you had been hit over the head with a blunt instrument. Times have changed, and, for better or for worse, language has changed as well.

During the Twentieth Century, and as a result of literature, theater, cinema, and television, we became acclimatized to shorter scenes and shorter sentences. Our concentration span grew smaller and our stamina fell off. We have come to expect that information will be conveyed quickly and in small bites. Dickens, with his six-line sentences, is hard going for some people: Harold Robbins, following Hemingway, got us accustomed to the six-word sentence. Here are two six-word sentences:

This is how people are today. This is what we have to aim for.

It's not easy. Our education taught us to cope effortlessly with forty-word sentences. We lawyers tend to think in longer strands than most people. We use grammatical forms jurors don't often use themselves. We use subordinate clauses. We use parentheses.

We have to learn *not* to use them. It takes practice. Focus on simplification. Start examining your own sentences. Count the words. Find out how many words your average sentence contains. If your personal word count is greater than twenty-two, start working actively to cut it back.

We are aiming for a balance here. We don't want to sound stilted, yet we want to make sure we are effortlessly understandable at all times. Take the kind of opening statement the factfinder is often subjected to.

"Ladies and gentlemen, I, as you know, represent the plaintiff in the case, Mrs. Mary Snooks, the case arising out of a most unfortunate collision which occurred on Sunday, August 9, 1987, at the junction between Caminito del Playa and Samantha Smith Boulevard in Santa Barbara, between a light blue Cadillac 1980 El Dorado, which was being driven by my client, and a dark blue Toyota wagon that was at the time being driven, with permission and consent, by the son of the defendant, who was currently employed by him and was delivering some urgent printed material to a customer for his father. . . ."

This is typical. And the lawyer has already lost his jury. They started to get anxious at about line four. The first thing they asked themselves was, "Are we expected to *remember* all this?" The next question they asked themselves was, "Are we expected to take all this in?"

As the lawyer went inexorably on, the jurors quietly began to panic. They realized it was beyond them to retain the detail, to follow the detail even—and they began to switch off. By the end of the sentence, they were uncomfortable and out of their depth, and already they were subconsciously regarding the lawyer as someone who was making life difficult for them.

This clearly illustrates the need for the Keep It Simple Rule, but it also leads to the next obvious practical rule:

Rule 26
Avoid Detail

It is one of the surest signs of the inexperienced advocate that he loads down his factfinder with too much detail. You see it again and again, and you see a glazed look come over the jury. If you overload them they won't *understand*, they won't *listen,* and they will *resent you* bitterly.

How should that opening have been done? Something like this perhaps:

"Ladies and gentlemen, let me tell you what I expect the evidence to prove. This case is about a collision between two cars and what happened as a result. It was a summer's day a few years back. Mary Snooks, mother of two, homemaker in Santa Barbara, was driving an old Cadillac. She knew the road well. As she came to a familiar crossing where *she* had the right of way, she saw a Toyota wagon. This other car was approaching its stop line on Mary Snooks' left-hand side. But instead of stopping, instead of slowing down even, the Toyota came right out into the junction. And there was a collision. Bear with me a moment while I give you a few details about that collision and its results. Let me summarize for you, in as few words as possible, what you are likely to hear from the witnesses in this case. First, who was driving the other car?"

Right? What have we left out? There's no mention of the month when it happened. There's no mention of the day of the week or of the date. There's no mention of the names of the roads, the model of the Cadillac, the year it was built.

We haven't stripped out all the detail. We've left enough for the jury to construct the clearest picture in their own mind, using their own imagination. And we've given them enough detail to imagine how *they* would have felt if they had been driving along that road.

But we have eliminated everything we could do without, everything that wasn't strictly necessary for our purpose. And what was that purpose? It was to tell the jurors a story they would want to listen to and be interested in, while at the same time stating the facts that would prevent a directed verdict against us.

So when I offer you as a practical rule, Avoid Detail, you may feel the rule can be extended slightly:

Rule 27
Work at Eliminating Everything that Can Safely Be Eliminated

Your case should be as lean as you can make it. It shouldn't carry an ounce of unnecessary weight.

Which brings us to a practical rule we have already met, when talking about the Dimension of Time, but a rule we didn't actually put into words.

Rule 28
Be Brief

Do not use up a minute more of your factfinder's time than is absolutely necessary. It works. It works incredibly well. You doubt this? I doubted it. We all doubted it. The practical rule, Be Brief, sounds like an encouragement to chicken out, not to do your best for the client, not to do a thorough job. It's not so.

Being brief requires planning, real preparation, intensely concentrated thinking. Covering all the points you need to cover without a single wasted word, making the impact you need to make as economically as you possibly can, is anything but easy. Getting ready to do this successfully can be hard labor. But it works and I'll demonstrate to you why it works.

Imagine yourself sitting on a jury. The trial lawyer stands up and does his opening. He tells you a story, a story that's easy to follow and that engages your interest. You can see very clearly why the case had to come to court. He's made you feel a wrong has been suffered that needs to be righted. But suddenly he's stopped. Just when you were comfortably settling in to the unexpectedly enjoyable business of listening to this interesting guy—he's done. *He has stopped before you've had enough*. He followed the rule of all good entertainment: *he left you wanting more.*

You are now in a state of looking forward to the next time that guy gets to his feet. When he does, he will have your total attention. But he does it again. Even before you settle in to really enjoying it, he's finished. And he does it again the time after that. He does it all the way through the trial. Then you come to his final summation and instead of being so brief, this time he gives you a little more. And even a little bit more is so gratifying.

By working the Brevity Rule in harness with the Tell Them a Story Rule *(Rule 22)* in harness with the Avoid Detail Rule *(Rule 26)*, this advocate has you sitting in rapt attention every time he opens his mouth. When you see it done properly, it's a delight to behold, and the contrast with the ordinary, run-of-the-mill advocate is amazing.

There is one last rule I'd like to share with you under the general heading of keeping them entertained. It's this:

Rule 29
Prepare Them for the Boring Bits

There *are* trials without any boring bits, but they are rare. Although you strive to keep your boring bits to a minimum, you can rarely avoid them altogether. How do you hold the jury's attention during a barren patch, during an investigation of what are bound to be boring details? The law court stops being good theater at this point. Is there anything you can do about it?

It's surprisingly easy. All you have to do is warn them in advance and then, during the boring interlude, make the occasional reference to time. The factfinder doesn't expect a trial to be all plain sailing. Both judge and jury realize that work has to be done from time to time. As long as you make it clear that you *recognize* the barren patch and also make it clear that you are doing your best to get everybody through it as effortlessly as possible, you won't lose their attention and they won't hold it against you.

So tell them in advance:

"The time will come in this trial, ladies and gentlemen, when I'm going to have to ask you to give your keenest attention to some rather complicated figures. I'm sorry about this but it can't be avoided. I'll help you through them as best I can, and I can tell you now this shouldn't occupy more than a couple of hours of your time. But that's some way down the road yet, and I'll warn you when we get to it. Meanwhile . . . ."

Preparing them for the boring bits is a specific application of a wider practical rule that says simply: Prepare Them. But we will come to that a little later. I'd like to finish with the theater-courtroom comparison first. I want to deal for a moment or two with this thing called *voice*.

This is something the actor studies carefully: we lawyers give it hardly any attention. We should. There are attorneys whom juries have difficulty in hearing. Others have such heavy, booming voices that jurors cower before them. Both kinds are letting down the client. There are a few obvious practical rules relating to voice.

First:

Rule 30
Know Your Audibility

Be sure that you know how loudly you have to speak so as to be heard. Courts come in different shapes and sizes. Ceiling heights vary considerably. Some courts have sound-absorbing walls, some ring like the inside of a bell. If you haven't already done it, practice using your voice in as many different spaces as you can. Get your spouse or friend to tell you how easily you can be heard. Explore your range of loudness and softness. Very important is to discover how quietly you can talk while still being easy to hear. This is because the quieter and more conversational your tone in court, the more effective you usually are.

The days of great oratory are over—at least for the time being.

People respond more, these days, to the kind of delivery that is conversational, informative and fairly gentle—and knowing your own audibility at this end of your range is essential.

Next rule:

Rule 31
Vary Your Pace and Vary Your Tone

If you don't, you will sound boring, and if your voice sounds boring, you undo most of the good you accomplished by putting all the other rules into operation. Listen to yourself on the tape recorder. If you can bear to, set up a video camera on yourself while in conversation with someone. Listen critically. Is your pace too fast? Even worse, is it too slow? What range of high and low do you cover? Is your voice nice to listen to? Is it comfortable? As I said early on, we tend to bashful about examining ourselves like this. Don't be. Other people are going to be examining you all the time in court. You don't want to be the last to know you have some irritating habit you could quite easily correct.

New rule:

Rule 32

Be Aware of Timing and Use the Power of the Pause

Ask theater people what makes a great actor and most of them say, "Timing." Good trial lawyers know how important it is. But inexperienced advocates are often so anxious to maintain continuity, to keep talking, to avoid silences, they overlook the question of timing altogether. Don't make this mistake. Don't ignore the dramatic impact that a pause can create. It's important to maintain your continuity, but that doesn't mean you have to babble.

If you haven't thought much about timing before, I'd suggest you look out for it in the better television presentations. The newscasters are usually good illustrations of the acceptable pace of delivery. As to the pause, check out Jim Lehrer on his PBS *News Hour*, or think back to Johnny Carson and Benny Hill.

Before leaving the subject of voice, let me give you a hint, important enough to qualify for rule status:

Rule 33

Be Very Careful about Raising Your Voice

For some reason I can't fully explain, when an advocate raises his voice in court, people usually wonder, instinctively, what's gone wrong with him. It's probably to do with the fact that a raised voice usually signals anger or frustration. Whatever the reason, I've seen it again and again over the years. Raise your voice and they'll think something has gone wrong for you. So beware.

Dropping your voice, on the other hand, has exactly the opposite effect. As a means of emphasizing something, it works wonderfully. This is why it's important to know the quiet end of your audibility levels.

All of these practical rules and hints discussed so far arise out of our focusing on the similarities between the courtroom and the theater. And we're not done yet. There is one last thing that needs to be mentioned before we move on. It concerns *movement*.

Americans often feel that the English courtroom, with its wigs and gowns and its scarlet and ermine, looks like purest theater. And, of course, that's right. But think about it for a moment and you'll realize that the English court is almost entirely *static*. The barristers are anchored to one spot. They either stand up or sit down. They don't move around at all. If a document has to be passed, it is carried by a black-gowned usher, the British equivalent of the bailiff. An American courtroom, by contrast, is a positive kaleidoscope of movement. Even in the federal courts, trial lawyers move around far more than they do in England, and this movement has to be carefully planned. If it isn't thought about it can cause trouble. Let's consider how.

Rule 34
Stay Out of the Well

The first thing to think about is the part of the courtroom known as "the well"—the area between the front of counsel tables and the judge's bench. In many jurisdictions it is regarded as a discourteous act of trespass for counsel to step into that space. Exactly why this is I haven't been able to find out, but woe betide the attorney who invades the well of a court where the judge likes to see the custom observed. Inquire before the trial starts how this particular judge feels about the well. Ask the bailiff. Ask the judge herself during your pre-trial conference when dealing with "housekeeping matters." If in any doubt at all, stay out of the well.

Next:

Rule 35
Don't Get Too Close to the Jury Box

The jury may feel invaded and trespassed upon if you get too close. Individual body-energy is a very variable thing and it's hard to guess how a comparative stranger feels about you coming really close to him or her. If you unknowingly invade their space, you may well stir up hostile responses which even the jury aren't consciously aware of. It's a risk and it's never worth taking. Apart from anything else, it may offend the judge.

Next, and closely related:

Rule 36
Beware of Getting Too Close to the Witness

You risk giving the impression that you are bullying the witness when you get too close during cross-examination, or identifying with her too closely if she is one of your own witnesses. Notice that I merely say, "beware" of this risk. I am not stating it as an absolute rule. See what other lawyers do in your jurisdiction and what effect they appear to have.

Next:

Rule 37
Plan Your Approach to the Witness Stand

You have to approach the witness from time to time, to hand him exhibits, verify extracts from depositions, and so on. Know in advance what route you are going to take, and always murmur at the judge before you move: "May I approach, Your Honor?"

I won't presume to advise you on how to choreograph your movements generally. If you follow the rule about using as many visual aids as possible, you'll find that movement arises naturally out of handling those aids. The only thing you need bear in mind is that your *every* movement is an *active contribution* to the Video Dimension.

You can sum it all up by remembering to *think choreography!*

Very well. That brings us to the end of the practical rules that arise out of the courtroom as theater. What we come to now is the interesting stuff, the rules that emerge by examining the *psychology of advocacy*.

CHAPTER FIVE

The Psychology
of Advocacy

Let's go right back for a moment to one of the first things we talked about—the First Dimension of Advocacy. By the time we get to court we are no longer digging for the truth: we are trying to get an *opinion* from our factfinder saying, "You win: the other side loses." In civil claims we sometimes want another opinion as well. "In our opinion, your client ought to be compensated in the sum of such and such." Very occasionally we want still another opinion. "In our opinion, the other side ought to be punished by being made to pay the extra sum of $*x*." In criminal cases we want them to say, "In our opinion, this case has or has not been proved beyond reasonable doubt." In civil cases, "It's our opinion that, on balance, this is the side that wins the contest."

Of *course* there's a search for truth going on in a trial, but it's not the main objective. Watching and listening to the witnesses, the factfinder is bound to be on the lookout for the liar. But trials often end up—usually end up, indeed—without any liars being unmasked. What the factfinders normally have to do is decide which parts of the evidence they prefer. An advocate's job is to lead his or her factfinder to a *preference* and thus to an *opinion*.

It's obvious, isn't it, that preferences and opinions may be very firm and clearly held, or, on the other hand, not firm at all and anything but clear. We are not dealing with black and white, absolute things here. As long as we win the factfinder's preference and opinion we win the case. The point to be emphasized is that preferences and opinions are often fragile, delicate things.

Your factfinders may arrive at their preference and their opinion entirely as a result of *thinking*. But that's not very likely, is it? We think. Of course we think. But we also feel. The process of getting to a preference and an opinion involves both—thinking and feeling. Even trained thinkers like us, in choosing between two conflicting witnesses, often ask ourselves what our gut reaction is.

In a trial to the court you are before a trained thinker: here there may be more thinking than feeling involved in the search for preference and opinion. I say "may be" because that isn't by any means certain. Judges are human too.

But with a jury, as with any kind of factfinder that doesn't have legal training, you simply *must* work on the assumption that their feelings will be operating *at least* as much as their thinking while they work out their preferences and opinions.

If preferences and opinions can be fragile, delicate things, human feelings are undoubtedly the same. And these are the materials that we trial lawyers have to work with.

Rule 38
The Materials of Advocacy Are Fragile

This isn't so much a practical rule as a fundamental truth that should be remembered at all times. Yet it's a truth that has never occurred to the majority of advocates. You see lawyers behaving as if their factfinders had no feelings at all, whereas it is the factfinders' feelings you should be reaching out to all the time.

Your job is to make them *feel*, as well as think, that they prefer your version. It is your task, in total honesty, to lead them to this. And if you take this as your starting point, all sorts of guidelines present themselves.

The first is surely obvious. You want to lead the factfinders: you want them to follow. Which will they follow more willingly, a person they like or a person they dislike?

So our first psychological practical rule:

Rule 39
Be Likeable

At least be more likeable than your opponent. Leave the macho, tough-guy advocate where he belongs, on the television screen. The nice-guy approach is infinitely more effective. When the nice guy occasionally gets nasty—as very occasionally he may have to—the contrast is tremendous. Be nice. If you are likeable, affable, and kindly, you will evoke all your factfinders' nicest feelings. They will want to believe you. Look at the presidency of Ronald Reagan if you need proof of this. His affability carried him through all kinds of embarrassment. Jurors have a disturbing tendency to find in favor of the attorney they like. So work at being likeable.

But be careful. Juries have an amazing nose for insincerity. If you just try to *act* nice, they'll smell you out. The practical rule isn't "Act Likeable," it's "*Be* Likeable." If this involves rearranging bits of your personality, do it. If you need it, get help.

You see, the truth is that we all have a nicest side. It's that version of us our loved ones know, that version of us we share with people we really like. *This* is the version we ought to take to court. Instead, most lawyers put on a cloak of grim seriousness, solemnity, gravity, pomposity, and leave the real human being somewhere back at home. Coming across as utterly *real* and genuinely *nice* works wonders in court. Apart from anything else, it tends to be so different from the norm that the factfinder cannot help but notice, and respond accordingly.

Now, that's a simple rule. Let me give you a more subtle one. I think of it as the Sympathy Rule.

Rule 40
Aim to Create Sympathy between You and Your Factfinder

Since understanding and following the Sympathy Rule brings such guaranteed rewards, I want to explain it carefully.

If you can convert a dozen unfamiliar people into a group who are sympathetic to you personally, you perform a wonderful service for your client. If they become sympathetic toward you, a number of results will flow:

- They will listen willingly.
- They will put the kindest interpretation on what you say.
- They will feel reluctant to deny you what you ask.
- They will feel inclined to overlook your mistakes.

If you want the clearest example of what a sympathetic audience can be like, think back to a kindergarten school performance. There is the audience of parents, hardly breathing as their darling kids appear on stage. Every mistake is forgiven, the tiny little voices break an otherwise perfect silence in which you could hear a pin drop, and the energy willing them to succeed is so real you could almost photograph it.

It's an extreme example, but I'd ask you to bear it in mind, then compare it with, say, a meeting of angry shareholders determined to have the chairman and chief executive off the board and preferably out of town. When I talk about sympathy, this is the kind of thing I'm referring to. You can regard the kindergarten performance and the shareholders' meeting as opposite ends of the sympathy scale.

As an advocate, which end would you prefer to be nearer? The forgiving, giving end, or the truculent, hostile end? It's amazing how many lawyers choose the rough end—as a result of their ignorance and sheer insensitivity. They've never paused to think about *sympathy* between advocate and factfinder. It's never occurred to them. As a result, their clients suffer.

It's obvious that a sympathetic judge and jury are better for your case than the other kind. Is it just a question of luck, or can you do something about this? Strange to say, you actually can get a flow of sympathy going between you and your factfinder and the technique for doing it is surprising easy.

Take a little time to play a mental game with yourself. Try to imagine what it must be like to be sitting where your judge is sitting, seeing what she's seeing, hearing what she's hearing. Try to put yourself as completely as you can in her position. Do exactly the same with your jurors—every one of them. Do it as they come into court at the outset and do it now and again right through the trial. Imagine yourself into the individual's skin: get behind his or her eyes. It takes virtually no effort, yet it undoubtedly accomplishes something. This simple exercise puts you in far greater sympathy with them and, somehow or other, they are subconsciously aware of it. The result is, they give sympathy back to you.

I make no claim to understanding how this exchange of energy takes place. All I can tell you is that the technique works. Try it for yourself. You'll soon discover it prevents you from making all sorts of mistakes. You won't say or do things that get their backs up. You won't, as so many lawyers do, get into a confrontation with your factfinder. You'll have a much smoother ride with them.

And you'll be less in need of the next and vitally important practical rule. You can think of it as the Rule of Equals and Opposites, but I prefer to think of it as:

Rule 41
Newton's Rule

Let's return for a moment to what I just said. If you pay attention to the Sympathy Rule, you won't get into a *confrontation* with your factfinder. Most trial lawyers go barging into confrontations with the factfinder as a matter of course. They create them all the time:

> *"You can't convict my client, ladies and gentlemen!"*
> ("Can't we now?" think the jury.)

"You couldn't possibly . . .," says the lawyer.
("Oh no?" say their faces.)

"You will have to . . ."
("Will we now?")

The rule is simple. You push and they'll push back. You pull and they'll resist. You demand and they'll refuse you. You insist and they'll turn you down. Newton's Law of Motion isn't just a scientific law: it's an accurate description of human response as well. An action almost invariably produces its equal and opposite reaction, and it's one of the most important practical rules of persuasion and advocacy.

If you think intently about this, you will see how to avoid trouble. Instead of demanding, you *invite*. Instead of telling, you *suggest*. You don't *insist* they look at something: you *suggest* they might find it helpful if they did. You don't pull, you lead, and you lead gently. Stick and carrot has no place in advocacy: it's exclusively carrot.

The more you think about Newton's Rule, the better advocate you become. It is the most important rule of all when it comes to the question of *persuasion*. Not only does Newton keep you out of trouble: it can be used to tremendous advantage.

"You probably won't feel that this is terribly important, ladies and gentlemen," will focus their attention remarkably. If you say something like, "I'm sorry, I'm not putting this at all clearly," you'll almost certainly get their unspoken response: "No. Go on. We're understanding you perfectly."

This isn't a subtle advocate's trick. It is a rule of human conduct. If you know and think about Newton's Rule, you'll relate to your factfinders far better, you won't offend them, and they'll listen far more willingly.

This is such an important rule that I feel it's worth giving you a slightly fuller illustration. Let's take a common situation that arises, again, in a criminal case—criminal cases often furnish the best illustrations. The line the defense are taking is that the police are telling a pack of lies and that all of their testimony is a fabrication. Macho trial lawyers normally slam into the jury in their final summations, telling them that the police were lying, the whole thing is a travesty, they can't convict, etc.

Do you know what the average juror feels when she hears that? The average juror has never had a brush with the law. The only time she had a real encounter with a police officer was when she got a ticket for a traffic offense she *had* committed, and, although he gave her a ticket, the officer was polite and even a bit regretful. To the average juror the police are the saviors, the people who protect. They are the good guys.

Tell the average jury that the police are the villains and you go against their belief system. It disturbs them: they don't want to think that. If you ignore Newton's Rule at this point you are likely to create a confrontation. But if you do think about Newton's Rule, you almost certainly avoid the danger. How about this as an illustration:

"Ladies and gentlemen, one unhappy thing about this case is that I've had to suggest the police have been deceiving us. Not a pretty idea, is it? Not something any of us want to admit, the thought that the police who look after this city of ours, who make it safe for us to sleep at night, might have among them officers who are willing to lie to judge and jury so as to get someone convicted, officers who are prepared to stretch and bend the law. We'd rather not think about it. Far easier to turn our backs on the possibility as we turn away from other unpleasant thoughts. Shall we do that? Shall we say, 'He's a police officer: he couldn't possibly have been lying!'? Or shall we look together, carefully, to see whether someone's been trying to pull the wool over our eyes?"

There's no risk of confrontation there. We haven't pushed once, we haven't pulled, and we haven't trampled on their natural prejudices. Far from it. *We've adopted their prejudices as our own.* We've been talking their language and they know it. We avoided all equal and opposite reactions until the end, and then we used them in our favor. "Shall we turn our backs on this possibility?" we asked. What can the jury silently reply to that except, "Of course not." "Shall we assume . . . ," brings an almost automatic equal and opposite: "No."

And we also suggested that someone may have been trying to pull the wool over their eyes. What is their reaction bound to be— "Well, they're not going to succeed!"

Think Newton. Let Newton become part of you. He'll keep you out of all kinds of trouble and make a real advocate out of you.

Did you notice another thing we were doing in that little illustration? We were placing ourselves firmly on the same side as the jury. It wasn't a case of advocate here and jury over there. It was a case of *we*, not *you*. Shall *we* assume? Shall *we* turn our backs on it? Were lies being told to *us*? It's an example of the next practical rule in operation:

Rule 42
Include the Factfinder in! or, the Rule of the First Person Plural

Think *we*, never *they*. The witnesses tell *us* not *you*.

> "And what were we told by Mr. Snooks? You remember what he said, don't you?"

Get this idea firmly established in your mind, and you'll begin running in harness with your jurors and, like as not, with your judge as well. When you are questioning a witness, you'll remember for whose benefit your questions are being asked—your factfinder's. Instead of bald questions, you find you are extending invitations. "Would you tell these ladies and gentlemen what happened then?" "Tell his Honor and the jury where you were when this happened."

You mustn't overdo it. It's like any ingredient that makes things tastier: it has to be used in the right quantities. But it should always be there. The factfinders must always feel included in as participants, rather than left to feel dispassionate umpires sitting on the sidelines.

The next rule was fleetingly mentioned some time ago, but let's examine it now. It's the practical rule which says, quite simply:

Rule 43
Prepare Them

We don't need to spend much time on this rule, because once stated it's obvious. If you have weaknesses in your case—and *all* cases have weaknesses—then make sure you are the first to mention them. Get to your difficulties before anyone else does. You will handle them much more sympathetically than your opponent. If you have an unattractive client or unattractive witnesses, don't let the jury discover this for themselves. Tell them in advance and as carefully as you can. Use a little Newton if possible. If you have witnesses with really weak points in their testimony, make certain you get to those weaknesses in direct examination. Do not leave them there for your opponent to make hay with. He'll do that anyway, but spoil it for him in advance. Take away the element of surprise. Aim to make the jury feel, when he gets there, "Oh, that. Yes, we were told about that."

You can say virtually anything in a court of law provided you lay the right kind of foundation for it. Prepare your way properly and you can exclaim obscenities! No one will bat an eyelid.

Let me move quickly on to a rule which summarizes a lot of what we've already been discussing. It's the practical rule that tells you:

Rule 44

Always Aim to Be the Honest Guide

In Chapter 2, when I was talking about the Third Dimension of Advocacy—People Don't Like Lawyers—I recommended that you find a totally honest, totally sincere way of presenting your case. As an advocate you are not a hired gun, prepared to do anything for the right price. You are a professional with professional responsibilities and professional pride. By the time the factfinders have spent twenty minutes in your company they should begin to feel not only that you are honest, but that they can trust you. More than that, they should already have started to get the feeling that they can trust you completely, that you are not going to dupe them in any way. By the end of the first day these people, who were strangers in the morning, must go away knowing that there was at least one nice guy in that courtroom they'd feel safe buying a used car from.

I can't give you a technique for accomplishing this. There's no substitute for sincerity and honesty and likeability. If you hold on to the practical rules we've been discussing and *are* sincere and honest, you'll establish yourself as an Honest Guide. What I can do is point out three danger areas, then give you three positive hints. First, the danger areas:

Rule 45

Don't Ask the Factfinder to Believe the Unbelievable

If you press the factfinders to accept something that is beyond them, your credibility will vanish in a puff of smoke. Any good you may have accomplished so far will be undone. You will be a tredecator—like a clock that strikes thirteen.

Rule 46

When There Is a Weak Point in Your Case, Don't Pretend that It Isn't a Weak Point

Admit it, and show the factfinder how you still ought to succeed despite that weakness.

Rule 47

Don't Misquote the Evidence in Any Way at All, and Don't Put a Slick Interpretation on Any Part of It

Now, three positive hints:

Rule 48

Make Sure that You Always Come Across as Being Absolutely Fair

Rule 49

Keep Your Objections to a Minimum

Let's think about this for a moment. Every time a lawyer objects to something she risks making the jury wonder what she is trying to conceal from them. "What are they keeping from us? Why?" Of course there are times when you have to object—either to the testimony that is being called for, or to the form of the question, or to something your opponent may be saying or doing; if you want to complain on appeal, you must make a timely objection.

So you have to make a rapid judgment. You have to ask yourself, "How important is this? Must I really object? Is it worth the risk that the jury will wonder what I'm keeping from them?" Sometimes you have to think very fast: it's not always an easy balancing process. But if you work from the principle "Don't object unless you have to" and keep in mind the dangers of objections, you won't go flinging them around for the fun of it—as so many inexperienced lawyers do.

And just one further comment on objections. It's usually a good idea to seem reluctant when you make them. The Rambo-type objector is great on TV, but not in the courtroom.

My final hint for keeping your Honest Guide status is this:

Rule 50

Take Great Care Getting Your Jury out of Court for Bench Conferences

There are times in every trial when things have to be discussed in the jury's absence. Rulings that can be dealt with quickly are usually handled at a side-bar conference: anything that takes time is dealt with in open court but with the jury outside.

Some jurors detest side-bar conferences. They know something is being kept from them and they often strain to eavesdrop. They are human, after all, and it should be obvious that you mustn't ask for any more side-bars than you really need.

Being excused from court, on the other hand, is something they probably don't mind—provided they don't feel something is being kept from them. A break to stretch their legs, to get coffee, to have a cigarette—these are all welcome *provided* the jurors don't feel they are being excluded from something interesting.

The inexperienced attorney often does himself harm at this point. He stands up and asks for the jury to be sent out of court in such a way they can't help wondering what they'll be missing. The Honest Guide, on the other hand, says something like this:

> "Your Honor, there's a question of law I need your ruling on at this point. Perhaps the jury could stretch their legs while we deal with it?"

Don't you feel that invites their gratitude rather than their curiosity? If the judge is bluntly insensitive and says, "You want the jury out of court, counselor?" you reply:

"There's no need for them to sit through a technical legal discussion, Your Honor. I think it's right they should be excused at this point."

Any form of words will do, as long as you are aware of the need to take care.

Before we come to the last of the psychology rules, let me give you half-a-dozen short hints—tips that ought to make life easier for you:

Rule 51

Demonstrate Your Competence to Your Judge as Early as Possible

Early in the trial, quote a section of some statute, refer to a specific bit of the evidence code or a scrap of case law. Any little thing like this will do and it sends a signal. Judges are burdened by so many lawyers who really don't know their job. A sign from you that you probably aren't one of them gets the right energy going.

Rule 52
Practice Listening Intently

In court we are so concerned with what we are saying and how we are saying it that we often forget to listen as carefully as we should. It sounds silly, I know, but not listening intently enough really is a danger, especially during our first few trials. We are so wrapped up in the difficulties of getting out our questions and feel such a sense of relief when we actually launch one at the witness, we often don't pay full attention to the answer. Intent listening isn't easy. It has to be practiced. Practice it.

Next, a hint to get you out of trouble. Although you'll be doing your best to keep it simple and use short sentences, from time to time you are going to get lost. Your sentence is going to get longer and longer until you lose your way. Most inexperienced advocates get flustered at this point because they don't know what to do. So it gets worse. The secret is to:

Rule 53
Stop Dead in Your Tracks as soon as You Realize Your Sentence Has Become Too Complicated

As soon as you realize any sentence is a failure, stop. When you start to get lost, say something like: "I'm not putting this clearly. Let me start again." Nobody minds. If *you've* got lost you can be sure *the jurors* have, and they'll be grateful to you for taking the load off them as well as off yourself. You can start over without any sense of failure. We all get lost from time to time.

Next: You remember the rule about not repeating yourself. It's important. If you repeat yourself and they got the point the first time, they'll feel you are insulting their intelligence. But how about those occasions when you feel you really must say it again? Tell them you are going to do it. Let *them* know that *you* know you are doing it. Acknowledge it. "Forgive me for repeating myself, ladies and gentlemen, but it's such an important point . . . ." If you give advance warning you won't cause offense. Nevertheless, bear in mind the general advice of Practical Rule 12, Don't Repeat Yourself, and use repetition only very sparingly.

There are, however, two important exceptions to the Don't Repeat Yourself Rule. One can be thought of as:

The Coffin Nails Exception

If, in cross-examination, you are lucky enough to get a witness on the run and you have a list of things which you know he is going to have to admit, then you can use one, repeating form of question over and over again. It's like a hammer, driving the nails into the lid of the coffin.

> *You knew that so and so, didn't you, Mr. Witness?*
> Yes.

> *Very well. Knowing what you did, did you this?*
> No.

Knowing what you did, did you that?
No.

Knowing what you did, did you the other?
No.

You can get a slow drum-beat going if you do it right, and juries love it, their heads turning from you to the witness and back again like the crowd at a tennis championship.

You can think of the other time to repeat yourself as:

The Mark Antony Exception

In your final summation (and in the rarest of cases in your opening) you might be able to find a short form of words that you can repeat like a theme. "For Brutus is an honorable man: So are they all, all honorable men." By the time Antony had repeated that four times, Brutus was on his way out of town.

If you can find such a theme, use it. But make sure it's worth hearing again and again. Don't try it out on your factfinder without having tried it out first on your spouse or friends and, preferably, on a teenager or two. When it works, it works wonderfully.

We just used the word "theme"—a kind of tune that can be played repeatedly in your summation. "Theme" also has another meaning for the trial lawyer.

Rule 54

There Must Be an Overall Theme to Your Entire Case, and You Should Be Able to Tell the Story in One Compact Sentence

"This is a case of a cynical corporation putting profit ahead of public safety."

"This is a story of a public utility being so inefficient, uncaring, and unaware that they committed environmental barbarity over hundreds of square miles of your county."

"This plaintiff is trying it on, exaggerating the results of her accident and gambling that your natural sympathies will prevent you from seeing through to the truth."

Let me demonstrate with a short series of illustrations from a presentation by Brian Monaghan, one of California's most successful plaintiff's attorneys:

"Keeping in mind that every piece of evidence in the trial should relate to the whole, it is absolutely vital to develop a theme which encapsulates the theory of the case to which all evidence should relate. Some examples: *Sanchez vs. Bay General Hospital*, 116 Cal. App3d 776 (1981), a hospital negligence case in which the plaintiff's deceased mother received relatively routine cervical neurosurgery and was released from the recovery room to the post-surgery floor in stable condition, but then was allowed to deteriorate to the point where she experienced brain death through aspiration of her own vomit. She remained in a vegetative state for several months and eventually expired when a tracheotomy tube was allowed to wear through bone, muscle, and tissue into the innomiate artery because it was unattended. In that case the theme was 'they ignored her to death—*twice.*'

"In *Bigboy vs. County of San Diego,* 154 Cal. App.3d 397 (1984), a case involving a dangerous condition of a public road, the passenger in the right front seat of the car was ejected when it lost control on a dangerous unsigned rural road. The theme in that case was, 'Dana will be a paraplegic for the next forty-five years because the county *wouldn't spend 200 bucks* to correct a condition that they knew was one of the most dangerous in San Diego.' While this theme is longer than I would prefer, if focuses first on the strongest parts of the case—the permanency of injuries and the minimal costs of correcting the problem.

"In a case involving a real estate purchase-leaseback-and-sale scam, the theme was, 'Mr. R_____ was a foreclosure savior who himself became a millionaire in two short years.'

"In *Tibbs vs. Great American,* 755 F.2d 1370 (1985), a bad-faith case in which the insurance company, when told that the trial judge had advised that they provide a defense to an internationally known rodeo cowboy who was defending himself without counsel in a brain damage case, stated: 'F_____ the judge, no California court is going to tell this company what to do.' The theme was, 'an insurance company above the law.' "

Entire seminars are devoted to finding the Theme of the Case. Just be aware that your case must have a theme, and get into the habit of looking for it from the earliest possible moment. Trying to compress the overall picture into one sentence will help. Ask yourself the question, "Why is this case in court? Why didn't it settle?" That will focus the search for your theme very clearly.

How should you plan the strategy of your case? How can you know what witnesses to call? How can you keep track of everything? How can you anticipate the difficulties you are likely to meet? The advice I give you now is the original Practical Rule of Planning, and it solves all those problems. It is divided into three parts:

Rule 55, First Part

As soon as You Have an Approximate Idea of What a New Case Is About, Sit Down and Write Your Closing Argument

Yes, write out your *closing* argument. Sit down and write what you would have to say to your factfinder so as to be confident of winning the verdict. Don't worry at this stage if bits of it are fiction. Just from what you know of the case, write out your ideal closing argument.

Then read it. See how well the available evidence supports it. At once you will see the gaps, the missing bits. Trying to close those gaps is the preparation of your case. When you think you are getting close, perform another exercise:

Rule 55, Second Part
Sit Down and Write Your Opponent's Closing Argument

This will concentrate your focus still more sharply on what you still need to do by way of preparation and on the weak points you will have to reach and deal with before anyone else does.

When all this has been done:

Rule 55, Third Part
Sit Down and Perfect Your Closing Argument

Your closing argument becomes the blueprint of your trial. It becomes a record of your progress through the case, a shopping list of all you have to do, a really foolproof checklist. The evidence you need and the way you need to present it stares straight at you from this final plan. It's an old, tried system that has worked for centuries, but many trial lawyers have never heard of it. It's a great method and I commend it to you.

So what is the last practical rule in this chapter before we turn to the examination of witnesses? It is the rule that tells you all the way through trial, but particularly in your final argument, to:

Rule 56
Show Them the Way Home

I had an attorney, Jim, telephone me some time ago. He had been to one of my seminars and he'd been musing over the rules. "You know," he said, "this is *the* practical rule. It subsumes all the others. As long as you remember to be likeable, Show Them the Way Home contains everything else. It's the supreme rule of advocacy."

I don't know if he's right. I don't know if you can say that about any one practical rule. I do agree there are half-a-dozen standing out from all the rest—Entertain Them, Tell Them a Story, The Sympathy Rule, The Honest Guide, Prepare Them, Newton's Rule—but can you pick just one rule and say it is more important than the others? I don't know. These fundamental rules are like the major branches of an oak tree. And I told him this. "Ah!" he said, "but Show Them the Way Home is the trunk of the tree itself!"

And in that sense, Jim was right. It *is* like the trunk of the tree out of which everything else ought to grow. Let me try to explain it.

Show Them the Way Home. What do we mean by "Home"? It's the verdict we are asking for, the goal we are aiming at, the objective, the only reason we are in court. Everything we have done has been done for this. All our preparation, all the depositions, all the interrogatories, all the research, all the motions. It's all been done in order to get that verdict. That's "Home."

Show them the "Way." What do we mean by the "Way"? This is the heart of it.

Your factfinder, whether judge or jury, arbitrator or referee, starts out as a stranger to your case. They come like travelers in a new land. Somewhere in this country is the city you want to take them to, the city called *Verdict*. You know their journey to that city could be a difficult one. If this weren't so, you wouldn't be in trial at all. And you have an opponent who wants to take them somewhere else altogether. Both of you are there, as the travelers arrive like tourists, wondering what kind of journey lies ahead of them, and from the outset you are like two tour operators in competition for these tourists.

The brilliant trial lawyer grabs all the tourists, there and then. He paints them a picture of an easy, enjoyable journey, through interesting countryside, over smooth, paved roads. He sells them his city as a place where they'll feel content to be, a place worth having arrived at, a place where they'll be so welcome, a place where they'll be more than just tourists, a place where they'll experience a new and exciting sensation: the pleasure of bringing *right* where before there was *wrong*.

And off they all go, with the other tour guide chasing along behind, desperately trying to catch up and never even coming close.

Many trial lawyers believe that a jury often decides on its verdict after it's heard the *opening*! The mind-set they get into at that point stays with them all the way through. Unless there is a catastrophe in the evidence, they never swerve. They choose the guided tour they prefer and stick with it. It happens. I've seen it done and I've done it myself. I've had it done to me.

The "Way" to that city has to be attractive and as smooth and easy as you can possibly make it. *There are bound to be obstacles and difficulties and it is your job to know in advance what they are and where they are.* Before the travelers arrive, you must have planned their journey so as to take them around the obstacles and so as to minimize the difficulties. Your tour must be designed to drive them through the countryside that will engage their interest and attention. The places where you give them a rest-break should be thought about with care, the route should be chosen so that a gentle stretch leads to a dramatic vista where they can ooh and ah before coming to another easy-going stage in the journey.

You can see what Jim meant when he said that Show Them the Way Home subsumes other practical rules. Entertain Them is in there. The Honest Guide and Be Likeable are obviously there as well. So is Preparation. Once you see what Show Them the Way Home is all about, it's obvious that it runs all the way through your advocacy.

But let's be specific. We can see the way it applies generally. Let's have a couple of examples of the rule in action.

Focus on two words: *easy* and *difficult*.

For the average human being, making decisions is difficult, far more difficult than the average attorney realizes. If you have any aspirations at all to being a trial lawyer you are, by nature, more decisive than the average citizen. Most people prefer to have their decisions made for them. If they are put on the rack of not knowing what to do for the best, they get agitated and distressed.

Your job is to remove their difficulties. Your task is to leave your jurors with a decision they don't really have to make at all—because it makes itself. You should be aiming to make it a foregone conclusion by the time they go off to deliberate their verdict. If you are doing it right, you should be striving, from first to last, to make it easy for the factfinder to decide in favor of your client.

It seems, doesn't it, as if I'm stating the obvious? Of course we should be striving to make it *easy* for our factfinder to come down on our side. But, again, it seems as if the average trial lawyer has never so much as thought about this. An illustration, again from a criminal case:

I once watched an English barrister make sure his client went to prison. It was at the sentencing stage of the case. His client had pleaded guilty at the outset, but all the other defendants had made a fight of it and been acquitted by the jury. Because the judge had seen the real villains go free, he clearly felt sorry for the only guy who had admitted his guilt. The only difficulties in the "Way" to a very light and lenient sentence were, first, it was quite a serious offense, and second, the man had two previous convictions from several years before.

The defending advocate could have said something like this:

"Serious offense, Your Honor, *and* it comes on top of two convictions some time back. These matters may make it difficult for Your Honor to pass a moderate sentence. But I'm in Your Honor's hands. I wasn't here throughout the trial and Your Honor knows far better than I can what justice requires in this case."

That would have accomplished a number of things:

- It would have been a public acknowledgment, made on behalf of the defendant and in his presence, that his offense was a serious one.

- It would have been an acknowledgment of the fact that the defendant had a criminal record and that this wasn't something that could just be brushed aside.
- These acknowledgments would have removed a difficulty all judges face when wanting to be lenient—the risk that a light sentence will make it look as if the court didn't regard the offense as a serious one.
- These acknowledgments would have removed another difficulty. The court cannot ignore a defendant's criminal record. If a judge passes a light sentence, it can seem as if that record got overlooked. Either way the public might be disturbed.

But with the kind of words used in our hypothetical, we are placing ourselves firmly on the same side as the judge. By acknowledging the problems standing in the way of a lenient sentence, by voicing them in public, we remove the fear that anyone will think the offense wasn't serious. We remove the fear that anyone will think the criminal record got overlooked. Simply by telling the judge we know about his difficulties, we diminish those difficulties.

And did you notice the use of Newton's Rule? "These matters may make it difficult for Your Honor to pass a moderate sentence." What is the equal and opposite reaction to that? If he's inclined to be lenient—as this judge was—his reaction could well be, "Try me!" or, "Sure, but you watch how I handle it!"

But what did the barrister representing this guy actually do? He made the judge's difficulties worse. He stood up in public and airily told the court this wasn't a serious offense at all. It was unimportant. Then he told us that the defendant's previous criminal record could be completely ignored because it had all happened years ago. Then he said it all over again.

I remember watching the judge's face. At first he looked bewildered, then angry, then hardly able to control himself. He was one of the nicer judges and he clearly wanted to pass a lenient sentence. But if he had been lenient after that barrister's presentation, it would have looked like he was agreeing with the nonsense that had been said to him. He passed a sentence of two years' imprisonment. Had it not been for the lawyer, the defendant would have been let off on probation.

Not knowing Show Them the Way Home can lose cases that might otherwise have been won. I got the verdict in a civil trial once, not because I had a stronger case, but because my opponent broke the rule horribly. All the evidence was in and it was finely balanced. There had been six or seven witnesses on either side, and there wasn't much to choose between them. Since I was for the plaintiff, I was afraid I hadn't satisfied my burden of proof and I was getting ready for the verdict to go against me.

Then came a gift from the gods. My opponent in his closing argument told the judge—we had no jury—that all my witnesses had been lying. They had been trying to deceive the court. They were all dishonest.

Just think of the difficulties that placed in the way of the judge. If he gave the verdict to my opponent, it would appear he was agreeing with him. He took the view, as I did, that all the witnesses had been doing their best and there was no intentional misleading. Now he was being asked to brand these people as liars. In rushed Newton and the judge reacted accordingly. What had been a finely balanced case now tipped in my favor. In his judgment, His Honor specifically found that the plaintiff's witnesses had not been lying and that, indeed, he preferred their testimony to that of the other side. Case over.

These are two fairly blatant examples, I agree. Show Them the Way Home is usually a subtler thing altogether. And techniques as such aren't needed to put this practical rule into operation. If you focus on the necessity for doing everything you can to remove their difficulties, you'll almost certainly do it right. Take time out to sit and think about your factfinder's difficulties. Only then can you try to do something about them. There, anyway, is the trunk of the tree, the last of the practical rules I offer you—practical rules that apply to *all* advocacy. If you think about them, merely bear them in mind, your advocacy will almost inevitably be of a superior quality. And when it comes to the question of examining witnesses, you'll find you already know a great many do's and don'ts.

So let's turn to that now, the examination of witnesses.

CHAPTER SIX

The Examination of Witnesses

Some years ago, during an air journey, I came across a short story in a magazine. I tore out a page of it and later got my secretary to type out a fragment.

> Suddenly there was tension in the air. He didn't understand it. She stood across the room from him, her eyes blazing.
>
> "Oh you!" she said. "Your trouble is you're a lawyer! You always say things in such a way that the way is more important than what you are saying."
>
> "What have I said, for God's sake?" he pleaded.
>
> "That's the whole point!" she flashed. "It's not what you say, it's the way you say it. You say things and ask things as if you've thought out in advance the answer you want to hear, and your questions always lead to you getting that answer." She was talking fast and hotly now. "Sometimes I don't know if you mean what you say or if you're just pulling strings to make me say something."
>
> "Give me an example," he said, abashed.
>
> "There you go again!" she retorted. And she swung around and vanished through the door, slamming it behind her.

Whoever the woman was in the story, she clearly knew one of the disadvantages of living with a trial lawyer, and she put her finger on the first and most important Practical Rule of Examining Witnesses. Let me repeat, but paraphrase, her words:

Rule 57

Think Out in Advance the Answer You Want to Hear, and Design Your Questions with a View to Getting That Answer

It must be hard, living with a competent trial lawyer, because the woman in the story has described exactly what we do. It's what we have to do—think out in advance the answer we want, then frame our questions so as to get that answer and only that answer.

Remember again our First Dimension: by the time we are in trial we are no longer on a search for the truth: what we are seeking is an opinion in our favor. The rules of evidence set strict limits on what the witnesses may say and what they may be asked. It's the same with any exclusionary rules that apply. And yet, it is on what the witnesses do say that the case will be decided.

Your success or failure depends on *what* they say and *how* they say it. Focus intently on that. It's such a simple truth it tends to be overlooked.

It is the advocate's job to *control* what the witnesses say and how they say it. The lawyer who can't control these two variables is as dangerous as a driver who can't control his car, a pilot who can't control his aircraft, a dentist who can't control his drill. It is you who are in control and nobody else.

So, if we re-phrase the first Practical Rule of Examining Witnesses, we have:

Think Control—
Know What You Want the Witnesses
to Say, then Make Them Say It

The woman in the story was absolutely right. This is the secret of all successful examination of witnesses. This is your fundamental objective. Let this truth flow into you, sink into you and become part of you. This is the secret of how to exercise the *control* you must exercise.

It will almost certainly affect your private life—as it affected the life of the lawyer in the story. Once you get into the habit of knowing what you want to hear, then getting the other person to say it, you'll find the habit almost impossible to break. When wives or husbands complain, "Oh, why can't you stop talking like a lawyer?" they don't actually mean that. What they really mean is, "Why can't you stop *thinking* like a lawyer?" It's difficult. As you grow in skill as an examiner of witnesses, you run the risk of becoming a lousy conversationalist. If you aren't careful, you'll find yourself pulling people's strings and making them say what you want them to say in everyday life as well as in court. Beware of this. It can ruin relationships.

We all have strings. We are all puppets in the hands of the right questioner. Even we, with all our education, can be led by the right series of questions. Those of you who watch public television may have seen a British comedy series called, "Yes Minister." I want to quote a snippet from this. A senior bureaucrat is explaining to a junior bureaucrat how to get any result you want from a public opinion survey. They are talking about reintroducing the military draft, or, as they call it in England, national service:

> *Now, Bernard, a nice young lady comes up to you with a clipboard. Obviously, you want to create a good impression. You don't want to look like a fool, do you?*
> No.
>
> *So she starts asking you some questions. Are you worried about the number of young people without jobs?*
> Yes.
>
> *Are you worried about the rise in crime among teenagers?*
> Yes.
>
> *Do you think there's a lack of discipline in our schools?*
> Yes.
>
> *Do you think young people welcome some authority and leadership into their lives?*
> Yes.
>
> *Do you think they respond to a challenge?*
> Yes.
>
> *Would you be in favor of reintroducing national service?*
> Uh—Well, I suppose I might be.
>
> *Yes or no?*
> Yes.

Of course you would, Bernard. After all, you've already told me you can hardly say no to that. . . . Alternatively, the young lady can get the opposite result.

How?

Mr. Wooley, are you worried about the danger of war?
Yes.

Are you worried about the growth of armaments?
Yes.

Do you think there's a danger in giving young people guns and teaching them how to kill?
Yes.

Do you think it's wrong to force people to take up arms against their will?
Yes.

Would you oppose the reintroduction of national service?
Yes!!

There you are, you see, Bernard. You are the perfect balanced sample!

Notice the following:
- The advocate knows exactly what she wants the witness to say.
- She arrives there by a *series* of questions.
- Each question in that series is almost guaranteed to get the individual answer she wants.

This is how any examination should be built. It doesn't matter if it's an examination of your own witness or a cross-examination.

Rule 58
Every Examination Should Consist of a Series of Objectives

Aim to get the witness to agree to A, B, and C, and then, *as a consequence*, D. You must know in advance exactly what A, B, C, and D are. You must know exactly what you want the witness to say—or to agree with.

Think of it, if you like, as a railroad freight train—a series of freight cars. Each one is an objective. Each one is a series of questions leading to the answer you want. To repeat the words of the woman in the story: "You say things and ask things as if you've thought out in advance the answer you want to hear, and your questions always lead you to getting that answer." When you get the answer, move on to the next car.

Decide in advance with every individual witness what your overall objective is. If it's your own witness, your objective is probably to draw out the story of what happened. If it's your own expert, your objective is to bring out his opinion and his reasons for it. If it's an adverse witness, you'll have other overall objectives, which we'll come to shortly. But know exactly what your objectives are.

Knowing your ultimate objective, you can then break it down

into your freight train of individual objectives and work at them one by one.

Deal with them all—each individual objective as well as your overall objective—by thinking, "If this, then that." "If such and such, then so and so." Design your questions so as to bring out this, this, and this, then invite the witness to tell you or agree with what must follow as a result. And what follows as a result is the very form of words you want to hear.

Going about your examination like this—with every freight car containing the answer you wanted, together with the reasons why you got that answer—you will accomplish something very special: to your factfinder your advocacy will seem *irresistible*. Why? Because your factfinder will have followed you every step of the way and will have seen the sure way you reach your objectives. If you can be irresistible, you are likely to win their opinion.

If you know your overall and individual objectives, work on each in turn, and demonstrate as you go along *why* you are getting the answers you are getting—then, surprisingly enough, you shouldn't find examining witnesses difficult. The reason why lawyers are often afraid of the task, and why so many of them are so bad at it, is that they don't know what they are doing. Analyzed out like this, it's a careful, step-by-step operation that no one need be afraid of.

But examining a witness properly needs an awful lot of preparation. It needs intensive thinking about. Planning a good examination can take a lot of time. Realize this and allow for it in your timetable. Don't feel inadequate if it doesn't come together quickly. Devising your series of questions which guarantee the answers you want is as important as anything in the case. It doesn't require vast skill or any kind of genius, but it does require careful thought and sometimes a lot of it.

When you are dealing with the examination of your own witnesses, you have an obvious advantage. You can prepare them. The rules permit it and, if you stick to total honesty in everything you do, there is absolutely no objection, moral or otherwise, to having a word-perfect presentation ready for court. Indeed, in view of the kind of preparation the American system provides for, it is your duty to do this.

When it comes to cross-examination, such preparation is, by definition, impossible. But exactly the same practical rules apply. Know what you want the witness to say and get her to say it. Know your objectives and plan your series of questions with precision. This way, you never lose control. But we'll come to cross-examination when we get to Chapter 8. What other practical rules are there, relating to the examination of witnesses generally?

The first thing to say is that we have already met most of the Rules for the Examination of Witnesses:

Be Brief—*Rule 28*

Entertain Them—*Rule 21*

Tell Them a Story—*Rule 22*

Utmost Sincerity—*Rule 4*

Don't Sound like a Lawyer—*Rule 11*

Beware of Repeating Yourself—*Rule 12*

103

Don't Put Words into the Mouth of Your Own Witness—*Rule 18*

Eye Contact—*Rule 8*

Give Them Something to Look at—*Rule 6*

Be Likeable—*Rule 39*

Think We, Not They—*Rule 42*

Get to Your Weak Points before Your Opponent—*Rule 46*

Avoid Detail—*Rule 26*

Keep It Simple—*Rule 25*

Think Beginning, Middle, and End—*Rule 23*

Listen Intently—Particularly to the Answers to Your Own Questions—*Rule 52*

Vary Your Pace and Vary Your Tone—*Rule 31*

Remember the Sympathy Rule—*Rule 40*

Always Appear to Be Absolutely Fair—*Rule 48*

Never Forget to Show Them the Way Home—*Rule 56*

All these are as important in the examination of witnesses as they are throughout the rest of the case.

But let me give you three rules that specifically relate to examination: They are the Never Forget and the Never Turn Rules.

Rule 59
Never Forget that the Average Witness Speaks from Memory

Pause and consider this rule for a moment. We are not referring to expert witnesses here, or law enforcement officers: witnesses like this usually come equipped with notes of one kind or another. We are talking about the average, lay witness, the person who saw or heard something and now comes to tell us about it. Focus on the word "memory" and realize what a variable, imperfect thing memory is. Consider how it usually works.

People see or hear something. They perceive it with one or more of their senses. Inevitably, they interpret what they have perceived and it is this *interpretation of their perception* which they store in their *memory*.

There are two opportunities for error here: first, their interpretation may be at fault; second, their recollection will almost certainly be less than perfect. What usually happens is that witnesses to something think about it. These bits worry them. They are uncomfortable. If you are trying to remember something, you want a complete picture, an *account that makes sense to you*. So you worry away at the edges, trying to make them fit comfortably with the rest of what you remember.

All this is pretty much a subconscious process, but everybody does it. It is an unusual person who can happily say, "This much I remember. It doesn't make complete sense but that's OK by me."

Most of us keep worrying away at it, trying to make total sense of our recollection. And in so doing, we rub off the rough edges. Only when we have done that, only when we have a recollection we are really comfortable with, do we fix that recollection in our memory.

But once we have shaped our recollection so that we are comfortable with it, then stored it in our memory, we tend to guard it rather jealously. Ask us to admit we were wrong and you are asking us to return to the state of discomfort we were in before we rubbed off the rough edges. Remember that this is almost everybody's subconscious reaction. We tend to regard an attack on our memory as an attack on us personally. Our egos are involved. We can get quite stubborn in defense of what we believe we perceived and what we believe we remember.

So:

Rule 60
Never Forget, You Are Not Dealing with Facts, but with What the Witness Believes to Be Facts

If you bear this rule in mind and also bear in mind how stubborn most of us are in defense of our beliefs, you will remember to:

Rule 61

Go Gently When You Attack a Witness's Recollection

If you are gentle, if you appear genuinely reluctant to be disturbing a fixed recollection, the witness is unlikely to get stubborn. If you can sympathetically show the witness that, in one respect at least, his memory *must* be at fault, then, provided you are always gentle, he may be willing to agree that he can't really be sure about anything. If you find one little crack in his recollection, and demonstrate it to him with kindness, he is quite likely to surrender completely. I've seen it happen again and again, and in this way entire cases can be made to fall apart. Be gentle with a witness's recollection: it has to be treated as carefully as his self-respect.

Now, the Never Turn Rule:

Rule 62

Never Turn to a Witness for Help

This rule has a general and a specific application. Generally, it cautions you to prepare so carefully that your control is as near total as you can make it. Never make the mistake of thinking that the witness will somehow compensate for sloppy control on your part. She won't.

Specifically, what can happen is this: the lawyer has not prepared as fully as he should and he doesn't know exactly what the witness can and cannot say. A question comes from the judge or perhaps from the jury. The lawyer doesn't know the answer and he blankly and helplessly hands it over to the witness to deal with. If he gets covered in horse manure at this point, he has no one but himself to blame. He has failed in his preparation. There is no adequate remedy for such a situation.

Now, a few hints of general application in the examination of witnesses.

This is:

Rule 63
The One Line of Transcript Rule

You have all seen a transcript. You know that one line of transcript contains between ten and fourteen words. It is a good discipline to try to make your questions occupy not more than one line. Of course, there are times when you can't accomplish this. Some questions are necessarily much longer. But it's an excellent thing to aim for, and if you always keep the One Line of Transcript ideal in your mind, your examinations will be workmanlike, easy to follow, and almost certainly more effective. If you do aim for One Line of Transcript, you probably won't need the next hint, but here it is anyway:

Rule 64
Don't Ask Compound Questions

"Were you at the junction and did you see . . . ?" is two questions rolled into one. It's obvious that you should ask only one question at a time, but lawyers are constantly offending against this rule and attracting quite unnecessary objections as a result. Don't do it.

Rule 65
Use Variety in the Format of Your Questions

You often hear an advocate make a statement that he hopes to turn into a question by an upturn in his voice toward the end. It's unprofessional and it can look awful on the transcript. There are four proper ways of forming a question:

First: A simple question—
Where were you on the night of June 3?

Second: A command—
Tell Her Honor and the jury where you were on the night of June 3.

Third: An invitation—
Would you tell the jury where you were on the night of June 3?

Fourth: A declaration and request for confirmation—
On the night of June 3, you were in Jake's Diner. Is that correct?

The last of these, of course, is a leading question. Use it with care. The other three, on the other hand, should be used constantly. It is one of the surest signs of a very inexperienced advocate, examining a witness, that he only uses the first kind. He asks questions but never extends invitations and never gives commands. The result is a stilted performance that sounds unnatural. Make a point of varying the form of your questions. I won't go so far as to suggest that you use question, invitation, and command in mechanical rotation, but variation of form is vitally important if you want your examination to come across as real and interesting.

And as a final general hint:

Rule 66
Beware of Demanding the Yes or No Answer

If you do, you risk sounding like a bully, you'll almost certainly offend against the Don't Sound Like a Lawyer Rule, and you may alienate both judge and jury. People know it's an interrogator's question, and they also know that the answer is almost invariably, "Yes, but . . .". If you demand a Yes or No answer and get a "Yes, but . . . ," you simply dare not brush aside the "but." If you do, you will be seen to be unfair and you will have abandoned your role as Honest Guide. It's terribly dangerous.

But it's tempting, isn't it? The "answer-this-yes-or-no" question is such a precision tool. What a shame it's too dangerous to use.

It's not. With a slight modification, you can certainly use it, and in total safety. What you do is remove the atmosphere of interrogation by adding in a little kindness and courtesy and turning your demand into a request.

"Mr. Snooks, would you answer my next question, yes or no, if you possibly can: were you in Jake's Diner on the night of June 3?"

By framing the question in this way, you are reasonable, you are seen to be reasonable, and you are felt to be reasonable by your factfinder. You've effectively asked the witness, "Are you capable of this?" and your factfinder knows that of course he's capable of it. If he messes you about with a "Yes, but . . ." answer after such a fair question, he's the one who loses status, not you.

"Again, if you possibly can, yes or no to my next question: did you see Rosie O'Grady there that night?"

Don't overdo it. If you overuse the gracious request for a Yes or No answer, it begins to be noticeable.

Now let's come to direct.

Direct
Examination

There are *two* technical rules applying to direct examination which are very important. They are easily and briefly explained, but they must be completely understood.

The Rule about Leading Questions

We've already examined the leading question and seen how it can devalue the testimony. And we've already noted that in all jurisdictions you are forbidden to use leading questions when examining your own witnesses. There are, however, at least five exceptions to this and they are as follows:

Leading questions by consent: You can always use leading questions if your opponent agrees. There are usually parts of a case where little is in issue. In order to save time and charge through these areas, you and your opponent may agree in advance that you can ask leading questions. Do take care, however, and permit me to repeat myself. It may save time and make it easier for you, but don't forget that if the testimony comes from you, the factfinder may regard it as almost worthless. If they feel the witness is only saying what you want her to say, this may infect their attitude toward the rest of her testimony—*and* toward you. Balance the advantages and disadvantages. Using leading questions by consent saves time and effort but may not be worth the cost.

Undisputed facts: Even without the consent of your opponent, undisputed facts can be brought out by leading questions. You know from the pleadings, answers to interrogatories, and admissions what isn't in dispute.

But the same considerations we've just discussed apply here. Don't lead if you feel the devaluation of the testimony might harm you.

Indisputable facts: Some things are so obvious and incontrovertible, everybody knows them to be true. You can lead these and there is no risk involved.

Getting a denial: Here you have no choice. You have to use a leading question. "Were you in Jake's Diner on the night of June 3?"—"No." The rules always permit you to ask a leading question so as to get your own witness to deny something.

"Laying a foundation": When laying a foundation, you *are* allowed to use leading questions. But what do we mean by laying a foundation? Think of it this way:

A witness can't tell you *what* she knows until she has told you *how* she is able to know it.

Illustration:

Mrs. Jones, you have told us you were standing on the corner of Van Buren Boulevard and Fourth Street, correct?
Yes.

What color were the traffic lights for Van Buren?
Objection!

Sustained.

What has been left out? The witness hasn't told us she was in a position to see the traffic lights. More than that, she hasn't told us that she *did* see them. Until she tells us these things, there is no foundation for her to say what color the lights were.

It's as easy as that, and it's an indictment on the profession that there are lawyers in the courts who don't know the rule. But if you *don't* know it, you could be reduced to tears by the objections you'd attract—every one of them sustained against you. You wouldn't be able to work out what you were doing wrong, you'd have the jury looking at the ceiling or examining their fingernails, and you'd probably never recover their attention.

So, how should that direct examination have been done, and how should the necessary foundations have been laid?

Mrs. Jones, you've told us you were standing at the junction of Van Buren Boulevard and Fourth Street. Correct?
Yes.

Can you tell us whether that junction is controlled by traffic lights?
Yes, it is.

As you were standing there, could you see those traffic lights?
Yes.

Could you see the lights that controlled the traffic in both those streets, or only one of them?
Only one of them.

Could you tell us which street that was?
I could see the lights for the traffic in Fourth Street.

As you were standing there, did you see something which attracted your attention?
Yes.

What was that?
I saw a blue Oldsmobile drive out into the junction from Fourth Street.

As that happened, did you see what the lights were signaling for Fourth Street traffic?
Yes.

Tell us what you saw.
The lights were red against the Oldsmobile.

Rule 67

The Foundation Rule: Before You May Ask a Witness to Testify on Any Topic, You Must Lay a Foundation Showing How the Witness Has Acquired Knowledge of That Topic

This requirement of laying a foundation runs all the way through the direct examination of witnesses, so get into the habit of thinking properly. Get used to asking *yourself* this coupled question: *how* did the witness perceive *what* she perceived? If you train yourself to separate all testimony into these two different categories, you'll find that you automatically obey the Foundation Rule. More than that, your examinations will have a rhythm to them, they'll be much clearer, much easier to follow, much more professional, and, indeed, more irresistible.

How?—What? How?—What? Always think in paired questions when planning or conducting a direct examination.

When laying a foundation, you *are* entitled to ask leading questions. If you think about it for a moment, you'll see why the rule is relaxed in this way: laying a foundation without using any leading questions at all is usually difficult, if not impossible, and the courts recognize this.

But take care. Even when you are *allowed* to ask leading questions, remember how dangerous they can be, and use them with caution.

What we have been discussing here, of course, is the second of the technical rules which have to be followed in direct examination. The Foundation Rule could have been dealt with when we were considering the Mandatory Rule in Chapter 3, for it certainly is mandatory.

Rule 68
In Direct Examination, Remember the Rule of Two and Couple Your Questions Wherever You Can

So what other rules apply to direct examination? At the risk of repeating myself, *all* the practical rules discussed so far. Every one of them. There's no need to go over them again. But there *are* some useful hints and techniques I'd like to share with you.

With the kind of preparation that can and should be done in America, the situation should never arise where you put an unprepared witness on the stand. Every witness you call should know exactly what you are going to ask her and what she is going to say. You should have explained the rule against leading questions and you should have made sure in advance she knows precisely what you are trying to bring out with each particular question. She must not be left in a state of wondering what you want her to say.

But suppose, for some reason, you had to call a witness you hadn't had the chance to prepare. Your investigator has discovered this witness at the eleventh hour, he promises you she's pure gold and safe to put on the stand, he gives you clear notes of what she can say, the judge refuses even a short continuance, and you have to examine the witness absolutely unprepared—using not a single leading question. Could you do it? A trial lawyer who can't isn't much of a trial lawyer, and if you don't know how, it's one of the most difficult things an advocate has to do.

No leading questions. The witness is sworn, she's told the judge her name and spelled it for the court reporter.

"Go ahead, counsel!" says the judge.

Mrs. Snooks, where were you on the night of June 3, 1987?

Objection, Your Honor! Counsel has just led the witness on a date!

Sustained.

You have, haven't you? You put the date into the witness's mouth. Suppose it's a criminal case and this is an alibi witness. The date will be of crucial importance, and you've just devalued every-thing the witness may have to say. So, how do you avoid this? Use a little lateral thinking. Let me share with you a technique that always works.

> *Mrs. Snooks, thank you for coming to court. Tell me if you would, do you know why you were asked to come?*
> It's about the fight I saw, isn't it?
>
> *What fight was that?*
> The one in Jake's Diner.
>
> *Are you telling us that you saw a fight in Jake's Diner?*
> Yes.
>
> *Could you tell these ladies and gentlemen the date when you saw that fight? And, for the moment, could you please just answer, yes or no?*
> Yes.
>
> *Is there some reason why you are able to remember the date?*
> It was my wedding anniversary.
>
> *Very well. Would you tell us the date when you saw the fight at Jake's Diner?*
> It was June 3.

That initial question, "Do you know why you've been asked to come to court?" never fails. Witnesses always know that, and they are so surprised at such an easy first question that, nervous or not, they give you an adequate answer. And once you've got started, you're away. Notice, by the way, the *foundation* we laid before asking her to tell us the date. How did she know what the date was?

The Murphy Method

I've already talked about the idea of pairing questions together so as to comply with the Foundation Rule, combining *How?* And *What?* questions—first laying the foundation, then bringing out the facts. If you do this, moving your direct examination forward by *coupled* questions, then, although I can't tell you why, this gives your examination a very satisfying feel.

There's another way you can introduce *coupled* questions into direct examination. It was identified for me by my old friend, Professor Peter Murphy, and I commend it to you. It simply recommends that you organize your questions into pairs, the first of them *general*, and the second *specific*. Illustration:

Mrs. Snooks, you've told us you were at Jake's Diner on June 3. Did you see anyone you recognized?
Yes.

Who did you see?
I saw the defendant.

Had you ever seen the defendant before?
Yes.

When had you seen him before?
He'd been at Jake's Diner the previous week.

And on that previous occasion did you see him do anything?
Yes.

Tell us what you saw him do.

Notice that the first question always contains a very open, generalized inquiry. Did you *ever* . . . ? Did you see him do *anything*? Did you see *something*? When you get the answer "yes," your next question asks for specific details.

Direct examination is one of the most difficult things to do really well. If you follow these two "rules of two," however, and get into the habit of moving forward, not with single questions, but in units of coupled questions—how? Then what? And generalized, then specific—your direct examination should be easy to do and elegant to listen to. Although this is a technique rather than a rule, it is so useful that I feel it merits a place in the list.

Getting documents into evidence

One of the most intimidating things about direct, until you know how to do it, is the introduction of documents and other exhibits. If you do know how, it's very easy and it gives your performance a dash of real professionalism.

Introducing a document into evidence is the moment when you break the practical rule about never sounding like a lawyer. At this point you aim to sound completely technical. Talk in a quiet voice and in a tone which is more or less expressionless, as you make it clear to the jury that this a pure formality which must be gone through. Your manner should be almost offhand, and you should quicken your pace. Remember the word:

MOASTE

This mnemonic will remind you exactly what you have to do. The letters stand for

**Mark—Opponent—Approach Witness—
Show—Testimony—Evidence**

and the following is an illustration of how it is done.

> *May the record reflect, Your Honor, that I'm referring to what has been previously* **MARKED**, *for identification purposes only, as Plaintiff's Exhibit 33?*—It may.
>
> *May the record reflect that I'm showing this same document to* **OPPOSING COUNSEL**?—So be it.
>
> *May I* **APPROACH** *the witness, Your Honor?*—You may.
>
> *May the record reflect that I am* **SHOWING** *the same document to the witness?*—It may.

(Now comes the **TESTIMONY**)

> *Mr. Witness, do you recognize this document?*
> I do.
>
> *Do you see a signature that you recognize?*
> That's my signature.

Would you tell His Honor and the ladies and gentlemen of the jury what this document is?
It's a letter I wrote to the defendant accepting his contract offer.

Does the letter bear a date?
It does. June 3, 1987.

After you signed that letter, what happened to it?
It was sent to the defendant by special courier.

Your Honor, I move that this document be admitted into **EVIDENCE** *as Plaintiff's Exhibit 33.*
Any objection?

No, Your Honor.
This document is admitted into evidence as Plaintiff's Exhibit 33.

Your Honor, thank you.

If you learn this formal routine by heart so you can run through it without thinking, you'll find it not only conveys your professionalism to everyone in court: more than that, it's a kind of staff you can lean on. Examination of witnesses takes intense concentration and it's sometimes very tiring. If you have half-a-dozen exhibits and run through this formal procedure every time, you'll actually find it gives you a rest-break from your intent thinking.

Refreshing Recollection

One last technique for direct, then we'll come to the rules that need to be spelled out for cross-examination. In every jurisdiction, witnesses are allowed to refresh their memory on the witness stand. Federal and state rules tell us what may be used, but they don't tell us how to do it. The main pointers are simple. If your witness forgets something, ask yourself if there is anything that might jog his memory. It might be his own statement, someone else's statement, an object even. Go through the following steps:

First: Ask the witness if something might jog his memory.

Second: Ask the court for permission to mark that thing with an exhibit number for identification purposes.

Third: Show it to your opponent.

Fourth: Show it to the witness and ask him to read or look at it *in silence*.

Fifth: Ask if it jogs his memory.

Sixth: Repeat your original question.

Very well. Let's come to cross-examination.

Cross-Examination

Now, what special rules apply here? We have already dealt with almost all of them. If I said nothing more and you put into operation all the practical rules discussed so far, you'd be a better cross-examiner than most of the competition. But which of the rules are most important for cross-examination?

Know the Answer You Want to Hear and Get There by a Series of Questions that Can Only Attract One Answer—*Rule 57*

The Freight Train Approach, Car by Car, Objective by Objective—*Rule 58*

Be Likeable—*Rule 39*

This rule is as important in cross-examination as at any other time in the case. You don't want the factfinder to start feeling sympathetic with the witness because you are giving her a hard time. If you turn nasty as you butcher a witness, make absolutely sure that the jury feels it's justified. Eye contact is terribly important here.

Think Beginning, Middle, and End—*Rule 23*

Particularly think about how you are going to end. Don't just run out of things to ask. It's terrible theater. Try to end on a high note.

Beware of Getting Too Close to the Witness—*Rule 36*

If you do approach the witness, because you have to deal with documentation, take care not to seem oppressive or bullying. Again, you want the factfinder's sympathy to remain with you: you don't want it to shift to the witness.

But there *are* special rules for cross-examination, and we'll examine them. Before we do, though, let's be very clear in our minds what cross-examination is actually for. Let's take just a little time to consider some practical philosophy.

What are the purposes of cross-examination? There are only two objectives:

First: If the testimony is damaging to your case, you want to show the factfinder that the testimony is *not safe to rely on* in arriving at the final opinion.

Second: Whether the witness is damaging to you or not, he may have testimony which is useful to your case. If so, cross-examination is the time to get that testimony out.

Those are the two purposes. There aren't any others. The second of these—getting out extra useful testimony—needs no comment, except for the warning, "Do it carefully." But the first purpose of cross-examination—showing that the testimony is *unreliable*—calls for careful consideration.

Let's stand back for a moment and ask the general question: *Why might testimony ever be unreliable?* Ask the question and the answer is obvious: the testimony comes from a *witness* who for some reason is unreliable. Our question therefore becomes: *for what reasons might a witness be unreliable?* And we can make a short list:

- The witness may not have correctly interpreted what he perceived. He may not have understood what he saw or heard. He may have jumped to a conclusion which was incorrect.
- The witness's memory may be at fault.
- The witness may be dishonest and intentionally trying to deceive the factfinder.

In short, the witness may be *wrong, forgetful, or dishonest.* And, of course, it may be any combination of these three.

Let's consider the possibility the witness might be just wrong. Why might this be? He might not have seen clearly. He might not have heard clearly. More important, he may not have understood clearly. He might have rubbed off the rough edges of his perception and stored something completely inaccurate in his memory. What should the cross-examiner do here? Surely, you have to discover exactly what the witness *perceived* and separate this out from what he *concluded.* You have to discover how far his perception went, reduce it to the hard facts. It is your factfinder, not the witness, who is supposed to draw conclusions.

When you do reduce it to hard facts, you will almost *always* find that those hard facts come in a surrounding package of uncertainty. If you explore that Perimeter of Uncertainty, you will get a lot of *don't know* answers. The more *don't knows* you get, the less reliable the testimony feels.

But that is an incidental benefit. The only way of discovering what hard facts the witness actually remembers is by mapping out his Perimeter of Uncertainty.

Once you know what the witness believes his hard facts actually are, then you consider his *forgetfulness* or his *dishonesty*.

How do you explore a witness's *forgetfulness*? Again, you can use the Perimeter of Uncertainty approach, asking him what he remembers of the surrounding circumstances. The more "I don't remembers" you get, the more unreliable the evidence tends to seem.

But when it comes to the question of forgetfulness, the best weapon of cross-examination is what the lawyers call a *prior inconsistent statement*. In ordinary language, has he given another, differing account on some earlier occasion? If you are lucky enough to have a prior inconsistent statement—in a deposition, or verified pleading, or in an answer to interrogatories, or in a statement to law enforcement officers—then you can ask the witness about this. Show him the statement, or whatever, get him to agree that his testimony in court is different from what he said on that earlier occasion. This cannot fail to undermine his present unreliability.

Two warnings, however:

First: Use your judgment, and don't waste time with little, unimportant inconsistencies. If you flog a point the factfinder thinks is trivial, you lose all your credibility as Honest Guide and no longer appear to be fair.

Second: When you get the witness to admit the inconsistency, *do not ask him how it can be explained.* Leave it to your opponent. It's a very natural human reaction, when you've exposed an inconsistency, to say,

"Well! How do you account for that?" Don't do it. If you do, the witness may give you an explanation —which may or may not be truthful—and you'll have muddied the point, perhaps even lost it altogether. It's far better, once you have exposed an inconsistency, to *leave it there* and move on to something else. You can be sure that the factfinders' human reaction will be the same as yours. They will be sitting there, silently asking, "Well! How do you account for that?" If that is how they feel, they are unlikely to regard the witness as reliable.

Come now to the *dishonest witness*, and realize that dishonesty comes in different shapes and sizes. Some witnesses are blatantly dishonest, others only slightly so. Some come to court with the outright intention of lying from start to finish. Others may be almost unconsciously dishonest, telling no outright lies at all, but slanting their testimony in favor of their side. Some experts fall into this category.

So ask yourself: *Why might a witness be dishonest?*

There are only three possible reasons:

- He may have a *direct personal interest* in the outcome.
- He may have a *bias* in favor of his side.
- He may be just plain malicious. This third category isn't common, but the first two are.

If you feel you can show the factfinder that the witness has a direct personal interest in the outcome, or a bias in favor of his side, then, clearly, this is something that should be explored in cross-examination. If you demonstrate this to the factfinders, they are more likely to feel that the testimony is *unreliable*—which is your objective.

Most lawyers never analyze cross-examination like this. They learn it by trial and error, but never focus on these underlying principles. They are so important. Have them somewhere in your mind at all times. What are the two purposes of cross-examination? What is memory? Why might a witness be dishonest? Is it self-interest, bias, or malice? Separate out what the witness perceived from what the witness concluded. Remember, all you are trying to do is to show that the testimony is less than reliable. Remember these half-dozen fundamental truths about cross-examination. Set them up like giant signposts in your advocate's mind. Keep glancing at them. Be aware they are there. If you forget these, you'll start to wander, and a wandering cross-examiner is a sorry sight.

Now, with these fundamentals as our roadmap, we can look at the practical rules that apply to cross-examination. They are all short. They are all easy to understand and remember, but if you don't know them—if you break them—you and your client could be in deep trouble. There are fifteen of them, but don't be alarmed at the number. Six of them are DO Rules; nine of them DON'T EVER Rules. Let's see what they are.

First, the DO Rules:

You've heard this one before and you must remember it:

Rule 28

Be as Brief as You Can Be

There is a special reason for this rule in cross-examination, quite apart from your constant duty to save your factfinder's time. Almost all witnesses get more confident and more effective the longer you cross-examine them. Why is this?

When you stand up to cross-examine, the witness is almost bound to be wary of you. At this point, you have an enormous advantage: *he doesn't know how much you know.* If he has been slanting his evidence, especially if he's been telling lies, he is afraid of you and of what you might have up your sleeve.

During the first five minutes, he is assessing the situation, estimating how dangerous you are. It's a rare witness who starts taking liberties with you at the outset. But the longer you go on without hurting him, the more confident he's going to get. The more confident he gets, the less easy he is to control.

You may be intending to lull him into a sense of confidence. It's useful to do this sometimes. But if that is *not* what you're trying to do, you should never let it happen. If you can get everything done with a witness during those first few minutes, so much the better. If you need longer, if it's one of those cross-examinations that can't be done quickly, make sure you use those first minutes to convince him that he dare not relax. All these things are encompassed by the Be Brief Rule.

This next rule is very simple.

Rule 69

Stop When You Get
What You Want

You know the answers you want to hear. You planned it meticulously in advance. You've got them. *Sit down.* You may be tempted to keep going. When things are panning out nicely, it can be such a great feeling you don't want it to stop. Recognize this as the danger signal it is and try not to yield to the temptation.

Until you get some real experience behind you, it's a good idea to:

Rule 70

Use Leading Questions
in Cross-Examination

It's easier to control the witness this way. You already know what he's said on earlier occasions—in deposition or in statements to police officers. You can exercise total control over his testimony if you use the fourth kind of question we discussed earlier—*the declaration and request for confirmation.* Illustration:

> *In June 1987, you were in Jake's Diner.*
> *That's right, isn't it?*
> Yes.

You were there on June 3. Correct?
Yes.

And on June 3, you were there at 9:30 in the evening, weren't you?
Yes.

You had arrived, I think, at about 9:15. Is that right?
Yes.

And you arrived in the company of a young woman. Again, correct?
Yes.

When you are cross-examining, there is little risk that leading questions will devalue the testimony, and they do keep the witness on a tight leash. When you've got some experience, on the other hand, move cautiously in the direction of using non-leading questions as much as you can. It is always better for the testimony to come out of the witness's own mouth. The ideal cross-examination is a combination of both leading and nonleading questions.

Next:

There are two ways of expressing this one. Think of it under the title that appeals to you more. It's the rule that says:

Rule 71

Pin Down the Witness

or, putting it another way,

Don't Spring the Trap until the Witness Is Inside

What does this rule mean and when does it have to be followed? Remember our overall objective: demonstrating to the factfinder that this witness's evidence is not safe to rely on. We can do this in three ways, quite apart from showing self-interest or bias. We can show that the witness's testimony is:

- **Internally inconsistent**—he's contradicting himself on the stand.

- **Inconsistent with what he's already said**—he's contradicting what he said before.

- **Inconsistent with other evidence**—he's contradicting other witnesses or the evidence of documents, photographs, and so on.

    There's a fourth way as well: once in a blue moon, you can show that a witness's testimony is plain incredible—not believable by sensible people. But that's a rarity, and I'm not going to take up time on freak situations. Let's stick to what you are likely to meet: internal inconsistency, inconsistency with an earlier statement, and inconsistency with other evidence.

    When you have one or more of these, then the Pin Him Down—Don't Spring the Trap Too Soon Rule must be followed. All it amounts to is this: before you face him with the inconsistency, *make absolutely certain he commits himself to the account he's now giving.* Get him to box himself in. Get him to close the door on himself. Get him to tell the factfinder that this is his testimony, no doubt about it. Get rid of all the ifs and buts. Close all the gaps he might try to slither through. Get him to commit himself, to pin himself down.

Only when you've done that do you produce the inconsistency and face him with it—if, indeed, you produce it at all. If the inconsistency arises out of his conflict with the other evidence, *you do nothing more.* Just save it up for your closing argument. If the inconsistency arises because he's contradicted himself, again, *leave it there.* Save that, too, for your final argument. You have nothing to gain by facing him with it except a dramatic flourish, and, even though you've boxed him in, you have no guarantee he won't be able to argue his way out of his inconsistency.

You only face a witness with an inconsistency when you have proof that he said something different on an earlier occasion. And even then, you do it with utmost restraint. The steps are:

First: Get the witness to commit himself, pin himself down.

Second: Get him to admit his earlier inconsistent statement.

Third: Move on! Do not, repeat, do *not* give the witness the chance to explain the inconsistency. Leave it to your opponent to bring out any explanation in re-direct— if there is an explanation, and if she has the wit to remember to do it. If you do anything other than move on to something else, you are playing with fire. We'll come back to this when we consider the Don't Ever Rules. Meanwhile, the last two Do Rules:

Rule 72
Keep the Record as Favorable to You as Possible by Moving to Strike Any Inadmissible Evidence

It's easy for an advocate to forget when a case really comes to an end. If you are for the plaintiff, the case ends when the defendant's check clears in your bank. If you are for the defense, it's when all process the plaintiff could follow has been exhausted. After the trial you are working so hard to win, there's a thing called the appeal court and above that, perhaps, a supreme court. Apart from winning that verdict, you have another job to do in trial: you have to *keep the record as favorable to you as possible*—because, if the case goes to appeal, the record rules everything.

When your factfinders have heard something, they can't unhear it. You can't, as they say, unring a bell. If the witness blurts out something you didn't want, the harm is done as far as your jury is concerned. But no matter what is said and heard at trial, the appeal court goes on the record, and if something is stricken from that record, then from the appeal court's point of view, it isn't there.

Never forget this. If inadmissible testimony comes in during your cross-examination, it is your duty to get it stricken.

How does inadmissible evidence usually creep in, and what should you do about it? If you are doing the job properly and holding the witness under firm control, the only way inadmissible evidence is likely to come in is when he gives you a *non-responsive answer*.

You ask the witness a question. He answers it, but then he adds something. Some witnesses try to make a speech in answer to every question. At the first sign of this, *break in on him*.

"Pause for a moment, Mr. Witness!—Your Honor, I wonder if you could explain to the witness that his answers must be responsive. And, Your Honor, I move to strike everything after the words so and so as being non-responsive."

Anything like that will do. But do it at once. If the witness still runs on, after the judge has instructed him, break in on him again, but this time ask the judge to admonish the witness. If he still keeps doing it, simply say at the end of his answer:

"Move to strike everything after so and so, Your Honor."

Your motion will be granted every time and the record will be as you want it in case you go on appeal. Move quickly when this problem starts to arise. If you don't, you'll lose control and your record may contain testimony you don't want.

If that was a rather technical rule, the sixth and last of the Do Rules is quick and easy.

Unless you are skillful and lucky, you are going to hit the occasional rough patch in cross-examination. You'll get an answer that knocks you off balance, that appears to damage your case. How you handle that depends on the circumstances. No one can advise you without knowing the facts. But the practical rule you *must* observe is this:

Rule 73
Ride the Bumps

Another way of saying it is,

Keep Your Dismay a Secret

Do not show by a flicker on your face that you feel you have hit a bump. Remember the Video Dimension. Don't look troubled unless you intend to—*Rule 5*. Remember the Honest Guide—*Rule 44*—and the Tour Operator. What are your tourists going to think if they see you turn white or appear upset?

Quite apart from anything else, they may not have noticed the significance of the answer. If you make a big deal out of it they *will* notice. If you signal your distress you make matters ten times worse. *And* you'll be breaking the mandatory rule that says, No Opinion from the Advocate—*Rule 15*. Show them your dismay and you are broadcasting your *opinion* on the answer you got. You lose all the way down the line. In the face of a lousy answer, *stay calm, look relaxed, and move on.*

If it's an absolutely devastating answer, you may like to use an old advocate's technique. In truth, it's an old advocate's *trick*, and I don't like or recommend anything that smacks of trickery. But it's very old, it's perfectly moral, and it doesn't involve dishonesty of any kind. Sometimes it works quite wonderfully. It's this. When you get that pole-axing answer, *look quietly pleased*. Say to the witness:

"Give me a moment. I'd like to write that down. See if I get it right."

Then write it down, telling him, word by word, what you are writing. Then look at him.

"Is that what you are telling us, Mr. Snooks? Yes? Very well. Let me turn to something else for a moment."

If you look quietly satisfied about the whole thing you deflect as much of the damage as can possibly be deflected.

Those, then, are the six DO Rules of cross-examination.

Come now to the DON'T EVER Rules, and start with a rule that's very similar to the one we've just been talking about. In a way, it's the same advice expressed the other way around, but it's so important it's worth having it both ways.

Rule 74
The Minefield Rule
alternatively expressed as,
Never Jump Back in Alarm!

Although your cross-examinations should seem effortless, they are often like a journey across a minefield. You are going with infinite care all the way, but suddenly your toe touches a mine. Alarm bells go off in your head. What do you do? You do *nothing that anybody notices*. Stay dead calm and act relaxed. You know you daren't go ahead, but you mustn't let anyone see that you've suddenly come to an abrupt stop. Think fast about what the witness said in answer to your last few questions. Pick something out of that, something unimportant and safe, and say:

> *Let me back-track a moment. Did I understand you correctly? You said so and so. Is that right?*
> Yes.
>
> *Very well. Let me turn to . . . .*

And you are out of trouble.

This isn't tricky lawyer game-play. This is you making certain that you don't inject your opinion into the case. If you think something's going badly wrong for you, keep quiet about it. You could be mistaken, and it's your factfinder's opinion that matters, not yours.

Rule 75
Don't Cross-Examine at All unless You Have to

A great way of destroying the impact of a witness is to say, "No questions, Your Honor." You'll know what a powerful effect this has when somebody does it to you. You've gone to all the hassle of getting the witness to court, you've done your best, and your opponent brushes it all aside with "No questions, Your Honor." The effect on the factfinder is real.

Ask yourself: "Has this witness done me any harm at all?" If he hasn't, think fast. Do you have anything to gain by cross-examining? You'll know your objectives from your preparation. You know what material you have to demonstrate to the factfinder that the witness is not safe to rely on. But do you need to use it? If the witness has done no harm to your case, why bother? If he has extra and useful testimony that you want to get out, think fast again. How useful will it be? Can you live without it? Weigh up the pros and cons. If you are pretty sure he's going to give you something good, then go for it. If you're less than sure, give him the brush-off. Ignore him. It's great theater if you can.

Rule 76
Don't Go Fishing

With all the rules you have so far, you're not likely to break this one. But breaking this rule is the sure sign of an incompetent attorney. Trial is not the time for discovering information. Cross-examination is not the time for picking about and seeing what you can find. It *is* a time for presenting planned testimony to the factfinder. If you are foolish enough to go fishing in trial, you deserve anything you catch.

The next practical rule is a close cousin:

Rule 77

Don't Ask Questions to Which You Don't Know the Answer

Go back to the woman's complaint in the short story:

> "You know what you want me to say and your questions are designed to make me say it."

You are working toward hearing what you want to hear, getting the witness to give you the answers you have planned in advance. With one exception, there's no room in cross-examination for asking questions when you don't know the answer you are almost guaranteed to get. And what's the exception?

You remember the Perimeter of Uncertainty, discussed at the beginning of this chapter. You are testing the witness's perception by finding out what its limits are. You might be testing her memory, her forgetfulness, by probing those limits. Here you are bound to be asking questions to which you don't know the answer. *But you aren't taking any risks*. It doesn't matter what the answers are, if you plan your questions with utmost care. Probing the limits of perception and memory, you are asking about things that don't really matter. They are only relevant because you are "testing the witness's recollection" and you never expose yourself to danger.

The next rule is an obvious one in light of everything we've talked about, but a practical rule of cross-examination all the same:

Rule 78

Never Ask "Why?"
and Never Ask "How?"

If you do, you abandon all control: you throw the field wide open. The witness can say anything she wants to say, just about. You can't cut her off by complaining her answer is non-responsive. Almost *anything* is responsive to a question that asks *how?* or *why?* Those words are to be avoided like the plague in cross-examination.

This rule, along with the rules about never going fishing and not asking questions to which you don't know the answer, highlights the contrast between cross-examination in trial and cross-examination in deposition. They are different animals. On the whole, deposition-taking is a fishing trip. It's a fact-mining operation: you are always asking questions to which you don't know the answer. That's one of the main reasons why you're there.

And it's because these two kinds of cross-examination are so diametrically different from each other that these rules are so important to know. What's the next of them?

Rule 79

Don't Open the Door

Back, yet again, to our First Dimension: we are not on a search for the truth at this stage of the lawsuit. We are making a presentation to the factfinder. The rules of evidence and the exclusionary rules are keeping certain things out. You want them kept out, don't you? If you do, then make absolutely sure you don't so much as hint at them in cross-examination. Don't come anywhere near them: don't breathe a word about them.

If you wander too close to evidence you want kept out, you risk *opening the door.* And what does that mean? It means that your opponent will be able to open up the whole can of worms in re-direct. The factfinder will get to know about all kinds of things you never intended them to see. And one of the official facts of human existence, just like the other Murphy's various laws, is that a can of worms, once opened, cannot be re-canned in open court.

That's obviously an important rule. Two short ones now, and then the last of the cross-examination rules.

Rule 80
Don't Let the Witness Repeat Her Direct Testimony

This rule addresses the risk that the more your factfinders hear something, the more they subconsciously embrace it as the truth. Many attorneys start a cross-examination by going over what the witness just said in answer to the opponent's questioning. If there's a reason for this kind of repetition, if, for instance, you are getting the witness to commit herself before springing a trap on her, then do it. But if you haven't got a good reason for it, don't do it at all. You have no excuse for rambling about in this way while you get acclimated to being on your feet and while you wonder what you ought to be asking her.

Next:

Rule 81
Don't Ever Get into an Argument with a Witness

If you do, you lose your status as Honest Guide, you lose points in the eyes of your factfinder—and you may lose the argument. Maintain your distance: remember, you are a professional, doing a professional job.

The last practical rule of cross-examination is a great one, worth saving for the end. Like *Rule 56*—Show Them the Way Home—this rule subsumes many others.

Rule 82
Don't Ask the Fatal Final Question

Take the following old chestnut as an example:

You've testified my client bit off the end of the victim's nose?
Yes, I have.

And this was in the bar of Jake's Diner. Right?
Yeah.

It's a long bar, isn't it?
I suppose so.

Forty feet, or more?
If you say so.

And it's got very dim lighting, hasn't it?
You could say that, yeah.

You were at the entrance end of the bar, weren't you?
Yeah.

And the fight took place at the other end didn't it?
Yeah.

Over thirty feet way from you, right?
Yeah.

And the bar was crowded, wasn't it? Twenty or thirty
people between you and the fight?
Yeah, about that number, I suppose.

How's he doing, this cross-examiner? Has he shown the factfinder that this witness's testimony is less than reliable? Dreadful lighting, obscured view, considerable distance from the event. Great so far. Listen, while he totally screws up.

So, how come you say my client bit that guy's nose off?
After he did it, he left the bar, and as he walked by me,
I saw him spit it out!

That's what's meant by a Fatal Final Question. It's fatal because it loses cases. It should be called the *Foolish* Fatal Final Question, because that's what it invariably is. It's a question asked in disregard of all the other rules. It's always unnecessary and it is almost always introduced by the forbidden words, How? or Why? It's a question that gets asked because the lawyer *can't resist trying to end up with a flourish*, because he can't resist ending up his cross-examination with a "There! Get out of that if you can!" And the witness gets out.

Don't do it. Don't go in for flourishes. Don't try to underline and emphasize the testimony. Don't ever give an adverse witness the chance to explain anything, unless you are positive what his explanation is going to be. Never ask, Why? or How? Get what you want, then stop. Never ask a question to which you don't know the answer. The Fatal Final Question is always the abuse of half-a-dozen rules rolled into one.

Now that we know exactly what we're looking at, let's have another illustration. They always make great after-dinner stories, particularly if they've happened to somebody else and not you.

This one happened in England, in a magistrates' court—the equivalent of a municipal court here. The advocate who screwed up is now a well-known high court judge, which proves we can all make mistakes until we've learned not to. It was in an old English market town in the dead of night. Two burglars, so the prosecutor said, were trying to break into a jeweler's store. The police sergeant who was the main witness testified he had come up to within ten feet of these guys and watched what they were doing before arresting them. No one, said the defense, could have got so close without being heard. It couldn't be true—it was unbelievable. The cross-examination of the police officer was designed to show this, and the defending advocate did a good job of it.

> *Sergeant, would you be good enough to tell us how tall you are?*
> Six feet three inches, sir.

> *And no weakling! Would you mind telling us your weight?*
> Tip the scales at just under twenty-three stone, sir.
> (over 300 pounds)

> *That night, wearing uniform, were you?*
> Yes, sir.

> *Helmet?*
> Yes, sir.

> *Greatcoat?*
> Tunic, actually, sir.

> *Boots?*
> Yes, sir.

> *Regulation issue boots, Sergeant?*
> Yes, sir.

> *What size were they?*
> Size twelve, sir.

> *Yes, I see. Size twelve boots. Studded with hobnails, were they, like the normal regulation issues?*
> (Pause . . .) Yes, sir.

They had a kind of small horseshoe of metal on each heel?
Er, yes, sir.

*And you say you approached within ten feet of these men
without their seeming to notice your arrival, Sergeant?*
(Pause . . .) Yes, sir.

Nobody else around was there?
No, sir.

Normal flagged pavements were there (British for sidewalk)?
Yes, sir.

*I mean, you didn't approach over a lawn or grass of
some kind, did you?*
(Pause . . .) No, sir.

Enough? Time to sit down? Useful cross-examination well-conducted? Get what you want, then stop? One question too many coming up:

*Well, really, Sergeant, can you suggest to the court how you
could possibly have got as close to the defendants as you say
you did without being heard?*
I was on my bicycle, sir.

Let's come to re-direct.

Re-Direct Examination

Re-direct is the most neglected corner of advocacy. Very few lawyers know what it's really for and very few do it well. So, let's look at it, briefly. First, what is re-direct for? Focus on three words:

Salvage, Clarification, and Massacre

Those are its three purposes. Let's look at them separately:

Salvage

If your opponent knows what he's doing and has some ammunition, he should be able to knock your witness about in cross-examination. You may be able to clean up her testimony in re-direct. If you know there are satisfying reasons why your witness said some of the things she said—reasons which your skillful opponent avoided asking about—this is the time to bring those reasons out. In re-direct you *can* ask, Why? and How? This is the first purpose. It's called *rehabilitating the witness*.

Clarification

At the end of some cross-examinations everyone is totally confused. If you leave it like that, the factfinder will almost certainly treat your witness's testimony as unreliable. All they'll remember is the chaos. Your job is to tidy everything up as best you can with quiet competence.

> "Let's go over some of what you've just been telling us, Ms. Smith, and see if I'm understanding you correctly. You said . . . ."

This is re-direct's second purpose—*clarification by restoring order and tidiness.*

Massacre

If your opponent, in cross-examination, did open a door, if he did open up a can of worms, now is the time to take advantage of it. You couldn't do this before. Now, as a result of his heaven-sent incompetence, you can. Enjoy yourself. That's the third purpose of re-direct—*making your opponent eat his can of worms.*

But be warned. And this warning applies to all three purposes:

Rule 83
If You Don't Do Re-Direct Well, It's Better You Don't Do It at All

If you do a weak or faltering re-direct, you play into your opponent's hands totally. You just emphasize whatever good he's done for his own case in his cross-examination. Putting it another way:

Re-Direct Must Be Done Confidently and Effortlessly

If you can't accomplish that, don't do it at all.

Are there any techniques to help you? There is one very important one. During cross-examination of your witness, take careful notes. Have a wide margin in your notebook, legal pad, or whatever it is you use, and as you note down what the witness is saying, scribble a big letter "*R*" in the margin whenever she says anything you think you might need to deal with in re-direct. This gives you at least a rough blueprint for your re-examination, and, knowing the case as well as you do, this is all you'll need to guide you through.

Don't forget, incidentally, that *you are back to non-leading questions now*. You *can* use leading questions to get out denials, and you can *also* use leading questions to refer your witness to things she has just said under cross-examination.

> *Mrs. Snooks, you said in answer to one of Mr. Jones's questions that you made a statement to police officers shortly after the incident. Did I hear you correctly?*
> Yes.
>
> *And he asked you what you had said to them. Correct?*
> Yes.
>
> *He didn't ask you what condition you were in when you spoke to the police, did he?*
> No.
>
> *I'd like you to tell us about that now. First, how calm did you feel when you spoke to the police?*
> I wasn't calm. Somebody had to hit me across the face to stop me screaming.

But apart from these two exceptions, you must remember not to use leading questions in re-direct. Incompetent lawyers always forget this rule—because they've heard so many leading questions in the cross-examination, they seem to catch the leading question fever—and it is disastrous for their cases to have their lame attempts at salvage and clarification pockmarked by a barrage of sustained objections.

Done properly, re-direct can repair all kinds of cross-examination damage. Done badly, it just makes everything infinitely worse. Don't do it at all unless you have to and unless you can be sure of doing it really well. Relax, stay calm, radiate quiet confidence. The Honest Guide is back in charge and about to restore sanity to the whole proceeding.

And when all is over and done, *don't forget the magic words:*

Unless Your Honor has any further questions of this witness?

Thank you for coming to court, Ms. Smith.

Your Honor, may this witness be allowed to leave?

Lastly, a point which is so obvious it can easily be overlooked: your re-direct *must* be limited to things that were touched on in cross-examination. Don't ever break this rule of court procedure.

And that is all I need say about re-direct. Think about it carefully. If you learn to do it well, it can be a lethal sting in the tail.

CHAPTER TEN

Final Argument

Closing argument, final summation, final speech—call it what you will. This is probably the most exciting part of a trial. This is where you are handed the magic wand, and where you can truly feel a linear descendant of the great orators of history.

Modern habits insist you use the language and the style of a *modern* orator, and a single Demosthenean or Ciceronian sentence would lose your listeners well before its end. But you have every opportunity the ancients had. That last speech to the factfinder is what it always was: an occasion when a speaker is given a chance to be spellbinding.

But there is *no* court, and there is *no* trial where final argument offers less than that opportunity. Your closing speech, those last words you say to your factfinder, should always be the most persuasive and most finely judged presentation you are capable of.

Trying to tell another advocate how to do a closing speech is, I feel, something of an intrusion. There are scraps of advice that can be thrown out, scraps sometimes so valuable they can change your whole view of the nature of advocacy. It was when I was agonizing over how to argue a case I first heard about Show Them the Way Home—*Rule 56*. But scraps are the most one should offer. If you try to coach someone into doing a certain kind of final argument, you don't help. The result is lacking in life and, most likely, comes across as wooden. You can't really teach final summation. It's one of the most personal things you'll ever do, as well as the most magical.

So, this is a short little chapter because I'm not going to presume upon your individuality. We've shared the rules together. You know what they are now and you've already, perhaps, begun formulating new ones for yourself. If you keep refreshing yourself on these practical rules, keep reminding yourself what they are, and keep thinking about them, you will have all the knowledge you need to produce a succession of magnificent final speeches. You know what not to do, and you'll find Newton breathing down your neck for the rest of your life. It's up to you now.

Just one *Don't*. Don't stand there and tell them everything the witnesses said. It's the biggest turn-off. Some lawyers seem to think it's their duty to start at the beginning and summarize every bit of testimony and other evidence in the case. Please don't do it, or anything like it. It's insulting to the factfinder, and they sit there thinking:

"Is this how it's done? I heard all this. Does he take me for an idiot? I suppose this is how it's done."

It's also very boring.

But you don't need to be told this kind of thing if you've read this far. *You'll* be telling them yet another story. *You'll* be holding up truth after truth and inviting your factfinder to agree that this is how everything irresistibly fits together. And emotion will be flowing.

I haven't said anything about emotion so far, but you are ready to consider it now. Emotion in advocacy is what brings everything to life. Emotion is what charges the moment with electricity and induces the pin-drop silence.

And there are rules about emotion in court—strict rules. Aristotle stated the first of them, thousands of years ago, when he was tutor to Alexander the Great:

Rule 84
It's the Factfinder's Emotion, Not Yours, that Matters

He formulated other rules as well, but I don't like them. He talked, for instance, about deciding in advance precisely what emotion you want to target, and contriving a way to stir that specific feeling. Like other ancient teachers, Quintillian, for instance, Aristotle strikes me as slightly cynical in his analysis. I wouldn't go so far as to castigate the ancients' analyses as dishonest, but they strike me as tricky and make me uncomfortable. The job we trial lawyers are doing is an honest job, and if there is to be emotion—as there must be—then let it be honest emotion, honestly created. It *can* be done, and it is done by remembering the next rule:

Rule 85
Emotion Follows Facts and Not the Other Way Around

I was examining the wife of a plaintiff on direct some time ago, asking her what her husband had been like before his world fell apart. She was telling us about things he used to do, how he used to behave. Then, without warning, I asked her, very simply: "Were you lovers?"

The court, which had been quiet before, fell totally silent. There was a pause that seemed to stretch itself out endlessly. Slowly, she raised her chin, and her eyes behind her glasses filled with tears.

"Yes," she whispered eventually.

In the same total silence, I asked her softly: "And how are things now?"

There was another pause.

"Different," she said, very quietly.

I sat down at that point, and my opponent didn't dare cross-examine.

There was no contrivance. It was a simple question. The facts were equally simple and they carried all their own emotion. With the greatest of respect to Aristotle, you don't need to target anything: all you have to do is give the emotion the opportunity of releasing itself.

And let's think about what we mean by "emotion." That's the old, Latin word. What we are talking about is *feelings*, and you are already familiar with the need to respect and go carefully with your factfinder's feelings. There is another rule that says, of emotion in advocacy:

Rule 86
Too Little Emotion Is Fatal: Too Much Emotion Is Fatal

But to you, this rule will be obvious. And since you know about the need to keep story-telling in the forefront of your mind, you'll discover for yourself that the easiest way to reach out to your factfinders' feelings is by telling them a story. All well-told stories evoke feelings of one kind or another: it's a human response and we just can't help it.

In every jurisdiction there are established jury instructions. In California, the very first civil instruction—BAJI 1.00—tells jurors, "You must not be influenced by sympathy, prejudice, or passion." In many ways this direction from the bench simply isn't realistic: of *course* the jury is going to be influenced by their feelings.

But suppose you find yourself representing the defendant in a case where your opponent really knows what she's doing. Suppose, for instance, that you were defense counsel in that case we touched on earlier in the book, in Chapter 3, the one about the little blue car traveling through the mountains. How does one respond to the plaintiff's attorney who has told a story well and who has stirred up all kinds of feelings on the part of the jury?

It's a rule of psychology and its equally a practical rule of advocacy. We must:

Rule 87
Acknowledge the Feelings that Have Understandably Been Stirred Up

Agree with them. *Identify with them*. Embrace them.

"What happened to Dr. and Mrs. Roe on that tragic afternoon is almost too painful to think about. You and I—all who were in court and who heard Mr. Turner's opening statement—were brim-full of sympathy. It's a devastating story, and if that was the only thing we had to decide, we could all pack up and go home. Because we are all agreed that we are involved in a tragedy.

"But this is also a lawsuit and you are a jury, and we have to do right by everyone involved. We have to try to do justice. And doing justice, doing right, means keeping your head while admitting that your heart has been deeply affected. Let's look together at the wider picture and see what else needs to be considered by a group of fair-minded citizens who are bound by their oath to do right according to the law.

"You will hear from Her Honor the judge that you 'must not be influenced by sympathy, prejudice, or passion.' But of course you'll be influenced, struggle as you may. We are all influenced. But with our heads as well as our hearts, let's take a closer, careful look at what really happened. . . ."

Before I end, let me just say a word about energy. Think back into a time in your life when you were really at your most energetic. It takes hardly more than a few seconds to do it.

Put that time at the top end of the energy scale and now do the opposite. Think back to a time when you were at your idlest, your most down, and your most unproductive. And put that at the bottom end. Now, without thinking about it, you know where you are on the scale at this present moment. Without any gradations being necessary, you *know* where your energy is this instant. It's a kind of invisible yardstick you just used.

When you are before a jury, remember that yardstick is in there with you. Every juror has his or her own yardstick, and so does the judge. Your job is to keep them in the upper half of the scale. Energy levels can be read. You can see it in people's eyes and you can feel it in the air. Keep the factfinders' energy levels up: all feelings depend for their quality on the energy level of the individual listener. Aim to keep your factfinders at an exhilarating level, so that at the end of a court day they can't wait for the next episode. It's not impossible. It's not even difficult. Just be aware of that invisible yardstick, be likeable, be totally sincere, and keep in mind from start to finish that, if there is an element of story-telling in everything you do, you're doing it right.

Written Advocacy

CHAPTER ELEVEN

Paper.

Pause and consider what it is. The Encyclopedia Britannica's opening sentence on the subject says this:

Paper Is the Basic Material Used for Written Communication and the Dissemination of Information

It's a good definition, even if an inadequate one. It reminds us of what paper *ought* to be used for. Let's take a moment, because this is important.

What we think of as paper began in China about 100 A.D. It was made, then, out of old rags, scraps of discarded fishnet, and the waste bits of, surprisingly, the marijuana plant. By the Eighth Century, it had become known as far west as Samarkand and Baghdad, but it took another 500 years before the Europeans got to hear of paper.

When they did, the public demand was enormous. By the time of the American Revolutionary War, the European papermakers were so starved of raw materials they had to place advertisements offering to buy old rags. It was valuable, sought-after stuff, and to an even greater extent than that other Chinese invention, gunpowder, it revolutionized the world—stirring up the minds of men to new awarenesses and new dreams. Without books off the printing press, new ideas could only spread at a snail's pace, and, without paper, there could have been no printed books. When you pause and think about it, you realize that, as an awareness-expanding vehicle, paper has been as important as the motion picture, as radio and television, and, as today's fast-developing marvels, the personal computer and the Internet. When we use paper, we are using one of humankind's great breakthrough discoveries.

Let's stay with the story a while. Because of the scarcity of rags, the papermakers cast around for a new raw material, and in the year 1800 they found one: trees. By 1982, more than 40 percent of all trees cut down were being turned into paper, and since then, the percentage has been increasing.

As well as providing us with paper, trees give us breathable air. Cut down too many of them and we are setting a problem for our children we wouldn't want to face ourselves. When you generate your next piece of paper, try to remember that. The lawyers of America could wallpaper the Grand Canyon every seven and a half weeks with the amount of paper they get through. When you are dealing with written advocacy, *this* is the fundamental truth that provides us with a new dimension:

Rule 88

Lawyers Use Far Too Much Paper

Why do we do it? If we can really understand the root causes of prodigality, we may be on our way to a cure. So, before we come to consider how to combine writing with the rules of advocacy, let's spend a little time considering *why* we behave as we do.

Engineering Language

First, a word in our defense. As every law student knows, the law is a vastly complicated subject—which is not surprising when you consider that it's the rulebook for a very complex society. Everybody's rights and everybody's obligations are set out in that rulebook, and those rights and obligations often depend on very subtle distinctions. Just try to explain the real nature of stealing to an intelligent teenager, and see how many "ifs" and "buts" you negotiate. The law can sometimes be as clear as black and white, but for the large part, it's numerous shades of gray. The only tool we have to distinguish between those shades of gray is a thing called language. We lawyers have to try to be as precise as engineers sometimes: in certain situations we have to aim for the same quality of exactness. But, while engineers have micrometers and machine tools and the help of mathematics, lawyers have to make do with words.

Most people never have the need to use language precisely. When they encounter someone who does, they understandably find it confusing, irritating, disturbing, threatening. They aren't used to distinguishing between shades of gray to this extent. Ordinary life doesn't demand it. Many people react to someone who seems to be splitting hairs by becoming impatient and hot under the collar. People would get equally flustered if they were forced to read engineering or scientific papers—my brother's Ph.D. thesis was incomprehensible to me after the first few lines—but they aren't forced to. The only time most people come face-to-face with deadly accurate precision in language is when they encounter law, legal documents, and lawyers.

We do have reasons, and something of an excuse for the monstrous complexity of the language we sometimes use—our *engineering language.*

The trouble is not that we sometimes use this language: the trouble is that *we let it spill over and contaminate everything we do. We don't work against it.* We tend to forget that the law belongs to the people, and that, particularly when we have dealings with non-lawyers, we have an obligation to make the law as comprehensible as we possibly can. They come to us for guidance and for enlightenment, and it's our duty to translate for them. We ought to be aiming, from the very outset of our careers, to be *user-friendly* in our choice of words.

There are bound to be times when you must resort to engineering language. Make sure such times are the exception, not the rule. Strive from the outset to express yourself with such clarity that a bright twelve-year-old would understand you. Any fool can make it complicated: it takes focus to make it simple.

The need for exactness is one reason why we are such a wordy profession. Another is the heavy weight of tradition. We are an old profession, and the rulebook grew out of the mists of history. When we arrive in the law, we are too new and inexperienced to have strong views of our own, and most of us start out working for a boss of some kind. If he is a traditionalist—as many lawyers are—we get led or forced into his ways. Many judges are traditionalists and can get irritated with different ways of doing things. Very often it's *safer*—and easier—to go with the flow, imitating the previous generation and thus staying out of trouble.

"Tradition" comes from two Latin words that mean a "giving across," and it's come to mean a "giving across" from one generation to the next. Just look back and consider how much you found already in place when you first came into the law. You remember the libraries, those walls of books? Do you remember how little you knew and how willingly you let yourself be guided into the "traditional" way of learning and of doing things? Have you ever stopped and wondered how much of a traditionalist you are yourself?

Most of us see no need to break with tradition, and we certainly see no need to reinvent the wheel. Almost every document you'll ever be asked to create has been created before, and there will be a precedent for it in the formbooks. It takes time and imagination to modify a precedent, and a certain amount of risk. It's easier to use it as you find it and get on to the next task. *Now that we have personal computers, the danger of just reusing what's already there is even greater.* If you can pull up a precedent that you can cut and paste to your present needs, what lawyer can find the time to do it differently? And why should she?

The next reason is that we get trapped by the *idiom* of the law. There are multitudes of phrases hallowed by centuries of use. "Last will and testament," "executors, administrator or assigns," "peaceably and quietly," "made and entered into," "force and effect," "unless and until," "save and except," "each and every." They are belt-and-suspenders phrases, and there was good reason for the repetitiveness of most of them—once. But they are terribly archaic now, and using them in this century is a bit like going to work in a plumed helmet.

That's the problem, of course. Every profession has a badge of some kind—physicians with their white coats and stethoscopes, engineers with their hard hats, psychologists with their irritating vocabulary—and when you at last arrive in your chosen profession, you have an understandable desire to wear your badge. You've made it and you want to show that you belong. You *are* an attorney. Why not remind the world every time you write?

These are just some of the reasons we are such a hidebound lot, why we use so much paper, why our style and method tend to lag behind the rest of society. Whether we are aware of it or not, every last one of us is carrying around many pounds of lead weights called "tradition" and "convention." It's not so much that we are afraid to be different: it's never so much as occurred to most lawyers that there might even *be* a different way of thinking and communicating and writing.

And yet it's the lawyer who *is* different, the lawyer who stands out from the crowd, who gets the notice. And the best cases. Look around the profession and check for yourself. Real stars—and there are only four or five stars in any branch of the profession at any one time—*all* do it differently.

This is the underlying truth of all superlative lawyering, and it's the same in every other profession. If you want to be outstanding, that's exactly what you must do—stand out from the crowd. You've got to be a bit different.

Rule 89

Good Legal Writing Is Easy to Read and Interesting, Accomplishing Its Goal in as Few Words as Possible

When it comes to legal writing, there's a guaranteed way of standing out from the crowd, and it's this: in relation to *any* document you author, make sure you can answer "yes" to the following four questions:

- Is it easy reading?
- Is it interesting?
- Does it work?
- Is it as short as you can make it?

If you *can* answer "yes" to these four questions, you'll do more than stand out from the crowd. Every document you write will be an example of written advocacy—letter, brief, pleading, or contract. If you ever draft wills, they'll be amazing.

Next time you feel tempted to churn out a piece of boilerplate, pause, and feel ashamed instead. Nobody reads it with any *interest*, you know. When it *is* read, it's only read out of a sense of duty. Such writing is the equivalent of boring the jury. It certainly doesn't get the reader's sympathy.

But let's get down to some details.

When you focus on the idea of written advocacy, you realize you are faced with a question that never arises in oral advocacy. When you are in court, inescapably in the Video Dimension, you should be engaging in advocacy full-time. You never have to ask yourself, "Is advocacy called for here?" The answer is always, "Yes."

But when you approach a written task, things are different. You have a choice, when you write, as to how much or how little advocacy you use, and it's therefore important to know, before you begin, what your objectives are.

Consider the question, *When is advocacy called for?* The answer is strangely simple: advocacy is *only* required when you want to persuade someone to a point of view.

Any fuller answer than that is only elaboration. There may be all manner of *reasons* why you want to lead people to a particular point of view. You may want a million-dollar verdict. You may want to get elected. You may just want them to feel happier. Comforting a frightened child is a good reason for using advocacy; making a loser feel less of a loser is another. Your objective may simply be that you like to be liked. Whatever your reasons for wanting whatever it is you want, remember that *you want something*. Until you have an objective, advocacy isn't called into play.

So, when it comes to written work, there appears to be a divide—written work where you want something and written work where you don't. One of them calls advocacy into operation and the other one doesn't.

But it's not as simple as that. It's not really an absolute divide. Even when you don't consciously want something from the reader, in reality you want quite a lot.

The Body Language of a Document

You want to be taken seriously, for one thing. You want to convey the impression that you know what you are doing—that you hold to certain personal and professional standards. Even a little thing like a badly folded letter may raise an immediate suspicion about your working methods. A letter with clumsy sentences and spelling mistakes will persuade any discerning reader that you are not a first-class operation.

Even though you may not "want" anything when you create a written product, you are inevitably going to convey all sorts of information about yourself. The words you use and the structure of your sentences say a lot about how your mind works and about your level of education. They say a lot about your focus and about your personal sense of style. The layout of your document says a lot about you as well.

Think of this as the body language of written advocacy, and realize that the rule is the same: since we all have body language, it's our duty to know what our body language is saying. Remember, too, that when you commit yourself to writing you are also, in a very special sense, entering the Video Dimension. All manner of subliminal advocacy—positive or negative—is taking place, and you will be judged accordingly.

Step back for a moment, therefore, and see what practical rules of written advocacy emerge from these fundamental truths. The first overall rule is this:

Rule 90

The Appearance of Your Document Is Vitally Important

Even when you are forced by the rules of the court to conform to a certain layout—as in pleadings or in briefs—you still have an immense amount of freedom in the appearance of your writing. Virtually all other documents give you total freedom to do it your way, and you should always bear in mind that the *picture* you create is going to produce a response—conscious or unconscious.

Shape, like music, can be pleasing or irritating, but it isn't neutral. A document that really pleases *you* in the shape of its layout has a good chance of affecting other people in the same way. Become aware of this.

Think about your own reaction to a solid page of typescript that is totally un-paragraphed. It looks daunting, doesn't it? Do you feel, consciously or subconsciously, that you have to take a deep breath and go for it, as you might go for something challenging? That's how most of us respond to a page of unbroken, unrelieved print. We are alerted to the possibility that this may involve effort, and our energy level changes accordingly. If it has been easy reading so far, the mere *appearance* of this particular page suggests that the holiday is over.

So, remember that:

Rule 91
White Space Is User-Friendly

Imagine your reader as a rock-climber, moving from one foothold and handhold to the next. Although she probably won't be aware of it, she will be *feeling* that the gap, the white space, at the end of your paragraph is the next handhold. If she sees a continuous series of footholds and handholds ahead, she will be far more relaxed than when confronted by a bare rock-face. Keep in mind the white handholds and, no matter what it contains:

Rule 92
Don't Produce a Paragraph Deeper than Four Inches

You'll break the rule from time to time. But, like the One Line of Transcript objective when formulating your questions—*Rule 63*—and the *22-word limit* for your sentences, aim for it. Your goal should be to keep your paragraphs less than four inches deep on 8½ x 11-inch paper. Your paragraphs will often be shorter than four inches, but try not to exceed that length.

Another form of white space is the margin, top and bottom as well as on the sides. The margin is the frame for your picture and, like all picture frames, it can either add to or take away from what it encloses. Experiment for yourself. Produce a standard letter with a one-inch margin on either side, then produce the same letter, this time with a one-and-a-half-inch margin. The second one has a look that is subtly different. The wider margin makes the second letter slightly more imposing: this letter asks to be taken slightly more seriously. Why this should be so would take too long to think through. What is important to remember is that:

Rule 93
Margins Have an Effect on the Reader

Be aware of this and be on the lookout for it. Decide for yourself, when you have the freedom to do it, what use to make of margins.

Rule 94
Lists of More than Three Items Should Be Vertical, Not Horizontal

Closely related to the *white space* rules is the matter of tabulations. If you produce a *list* of more than three items, *do it vertically, not horizontally*. This is because it is easier to scan a list when the separation of the items is clear, and because vertical listing involves, quite literally, taking a fresh look at each item separately. In a horizontal line, your eyes take in several items in one long sweep. In a vertical list, you move your eyes before each item. Consider the following paragraph from a contract:

WHEREAS parties of the second part have made funds available to Malvolio Hosiery Inc. in the amount of $156,873.00 in order that said corporation may properly pay such things as withholding taxes, payroll, purchase of additional yarn and trimmings as necessary, advertising, hookup to the regional sewer plant, making insurance premiums current, legal fees, keeping equipment payment current, together with any and all other items which might be due by the said corporation during its normal course of business; and . . .

Apart from being an untidy old plumed helmet, this recital is uphill work because of its list. Look how easily it can be improved:

At the request of the borrowers, and by way of a loan to them, the lenders have paid the sum of $156,873.00 to Malvolio Hosiery Inc. so that this corporation could meet its operating expenses, including in particular the following:

> (a) payroll
>
> (b) withholding taxes
>
> (c) insurance premiums
>
> (d) time payments on equipment
>
> (e) legal fees
>
> (f) purchase of raw materials
>
> (g) advertising
>
> (h) hookup to regional sewer system

Now ask yourself which lawyer you would want as *your* attorney—the one who wrote the first version, or the second? Every time you put pen to paper you are telling your reader what kind of mind you have, how effective you are likely to be and—and this is important—how *easy or difficult* you are likely to be to deal with. You are engaging in self-advertisement.

Tabulations are enormously helpful in all kinds of documents, and you shouldn't be reluctant to use them, even in letters. Use them whenever they promise to make your reader's task easier. But remember the bare rock-face of an un-paragraphed page: if a tabulation is too long, it will have the same daunting effect. The four-inch limit is a useful guideline with tabulations as well as with paragraphs. The rule is, therefore, use tabulations, but with care.

Simply glancing at your document now, well-framed, effortlessly paragraphed and with the occasional neat tabulation, the reader is instantly aware that this is a crafted product. Layout alone can attract subliminal respect, and if you have your reader's respect before he even starts to read, your advocacy so far will have been effective. Is there anything else you can do to add to the craftsmanship of your layout?

There are two other things I suggest, one obvious and one much less so.

Rule 95
Use Headings

When you use headings in briefs, follow the four-inch rule again. Headings are always centered in a brief. If a particular heading contains more words than can fit into a four-inch line, divide it up into two lines or more. Lengthy headings are almost self-defeating, though sometimes they are difficult to avoid. Turn them into a four-inch-wide "box." Whether you underline them or not is a matter for you, but boxed headings add to the crisp appearance of the document.

If you can print both serif fonts, such as Times Roman, and sans serif fonts, such as Helvetica, consider using the sans serif font for headings and the serif font for text.

The less obvious hint is this:

Rule 96
Consider Incorporating
Diagrams into Your Writing

This practical rule is a special application of *Rule 7*—Use All Kinds of Visual Aids. In briefs and letters, diagrams are unexpected. Yet the old adage about a picture being worth a thousand words is true in legal documents as elsewhere. It's a comment on our dead-weight conservatism that so very few lawyers make a point of using pictures when writing a brief. You want to be outstanding? Use diagrams.

In all but the simplest cases, the first difficulty the reader grapples with is the problem of who's who and who did what to whom. Yet it's easy to show relationships at a glance by using a diagram. You may have had to make a diagram for your own use, so as to understand the case. If it helped you, it will help your reader.

There are a variety of computer programs that draw diagrams, and they're affordable. These programs allow you to draw any chart or diagram you can devise, and their palettes of possibilities really stimulate you to more focused thinking. You are taking real advantage of the Video Dimension, after all.

Put yourself in the position of the judge who must look at your brief. I say "look at" rather than "read" to reflect the realities of life. I know judges who are deeply offended at the suggestion they don't read every word, and I know others who frankly admit that when the going gets tough they stop reading everything and start to skim instead. Reading briefs is more often than not hard work. They are usually full of convoluted language and footnotes, and they demand that you stay consciously focused if you want to wring understanding out of them.

Now imagine how your same judge feels when, suddenly, here is a brief that starts with an arresting paragraph, then moves straight to a brilliantly clear diagram, showing who did what to whom, and a lot more besides. This brief is different—it's imaginative and it's immensely helpful. What will the judge be feeling as he turns the page?

It's been said that you have a *nanosecond* in which to grab a judge's interested attention. Offer him something interesting in that nanosecond, and you are away. After that, all you have to do is hold him. Diagrams work wonders.

Enough, then, about the layout of your document. Let's come now to:

Pace and Movement

Think of the last time you found a book you couldn't put down, a book you had to read fast from cover to cover.

Now go to the opposite polarity and try to remember the slowest, densest reading you ever did. And now think about movement and pace.

There's great pleasure to be got out of a deep, slow-moving book—if you have the luxury of time, and if you're in the right mood. But if your workload means you have to read fast and steadily just to keep abreast, the last thing you need is writing that slows you down.

Ideally, you want the pace of the writing to mesh with the pace at which you normally like to read.

Everyone slows down a little when they start to get interested, but you can safely assume that most judges and lawyers tend to read fairly fast. Observe yourself for a minute or two, and note your reading pace. But before you do, read this:

"As in the structure of the plot, so too in the portraiture of character, the poet should always aim either at the necessary or the probable. Thus, a person of a given character should speak or act in a given way, by the rule either of necessity or probability; just as this event should follow that with probable consequence. It is therefore evident that the unraveling of the plot, no less than the complication, must be brought about by the plot itself, and not by machinery—as in the *Medea*, or in the Return of the Greeks in the *Iliad*."

Notice the pace you are moving at now? You have just been reading a passage of lucid language, expressing the essence of a perfectly presented case—written by Aristotle himself. And you have slowed down. Did the change of pace jar you at all? Did it seem as if we were losing power back there?

Rule 97
Write at the Pace of a Brisk Walk

When you are writing for another lawyer—and this means everyone from supreme courts, trial judges and judges' clerks, to your opponents, boss, if you have one, and fellow attorneys—you *must* move at a proper pace. It's not a run, it's not even a trot. It's a brisk walk, but it's a brisk walk that doesn't ease up.

When you are writing to a different kind of professional—expert, doctor, engineer—you can go a little slower, but not much. Writing to the client, or to witnesses, calls for a different pace altogether.

(How you write to a client depends on your objectives. Identify what those objectives are and how you want to come across, remember your body language, and start writing—at whatever pace you feel is appropriate.)

But how do you write at the pace of a brisk walk? Try the following slate of techniques and see how well they work.

- Remove all possible obstacles. Wage war on footnotes. Keep brackets to an absolute minimum. Don't interrupt the *flow* with anything that isn't vitally necessary.
- When your sentence breaks the 22-word limit, know by what margin you exceed it.
- Make regular use of six-word sentences.
- Vary the length of your sentences.
- Strip out detail—if you really need detail, tack it on later in the form of exhibits.
- Write English, not legalese.
- Make your sentences effortlessly understandable at first reading.

Follow these guidelines, and the pace of your writing will almost certainly take care of itself.

Now let's turn to *movement*. This is closely related to pace, but it's not the same thing.

In any written task, you have a certain amount of ground to cover. In a brief, for instance, you have to state the background facts, say what you want, and set out the reasons why you should prevail. If you spend too long on any one part, your movement slows down and your reader begins to feel burdened—no matter what your pace. There must always be a feeling of *direction* in your writing. Think why.

As usual, we're talking about normal human responses, responses that happen without thinking. Remember "You can't convict my client—you wanna bet?" The dangers of *subconscious* responses are out there all the time, and the more you are tuned in to how normal humans feel and react, the better advocate you'll be.

When we are on a journey, we like knowing how far we've traveled. One of the reason many people find air travel boring is that they have no meaningful landmarks: they never see that they have progressed to significant points along the way. Even at a window seat, the sense of getting somewhere is slowed down by the height. Low flying is exhilarating because you are constantly aware that you are moving, *progressing swiftly.*

One of the things that really interferes with a sense of movement is *untidy chronology.* For all kinds of reasons, we expect an account to start at the beginning and then move forward in time. This is important enough to be stated as a rule:

Rule 98
Pay Great Respect to Chronology in Your Writing

Note the words, "we *expect* an account to start at the beginning and move forward in time." If you ever mishandle *your reader's expectations,* you create a sense of puzzlement, and no matter how short-lived that sense of puzzlement, it is disturbing. It's like hitting a pot-hole. If you are forced to depart from normal chronology, or if you think it will improve the quality of your story-telling to use a flashback or a leap ahead, follow the practical rule: Prepare Them—*Rule 43*.

Warn them in advance and tell them briefly why you are disturbing the expected flow.

You must think *movement* all the way through your writing. You should give *assurances*, sprinkled here and there, that you are moving on. Headings are very helpful because they act as landmarks. Be careful not to space them too far apart. If you use the occasional phrase to remind your reader that you know how valuable her time is, you sustain her sense of movement. *Time*—our familiar Fourth Dimension—is as important on paper as it is in court.

"Turning briefly to the question of . . ."

"Moving on to the matter of . . ."

"So much for the background. Coming now to the reasons for this motion . . ."

Phrases like these speed the reader's progress. They also act as links, easing your reader from one part of your writing to the next. Don't make the mistake, when you come to the end of one part, of finishing in such a way as to suggest finality. End with a sign-post to the next part. Finality should only come at the end of your document.

Your writing's pace and movement, along with its gratifying layout and attractive body language, may very well go unnoticed. But you will have significantly raised your reader's subconscious *sense of satisfaction*, and, although she may not even be aware of it, she will be reading with sharpened focus and interest.

Now, let's come back to the words at the beginning of this chapter, the Britannica definition of paper.

Paper Is the Basic Material Used for Written Communication and the Dissemination of Information

The key words there are "communication" and "dissemination." If you are going into politics, you'll need to be expert at both. If you intend to stick to lawyering, you won't do much disseminating because you won't need to. An outstandingly good attorney, as skillful and convincing on paper as he is in court, never lacks clients and cases. His or her quickly-made reputation does all the disseminating necessary.

Communication, as you don't need to be reminded, is what advocacy is all about.

And that's what this chapter is all about. So far, if you think about it, we have been considering the way in which the Sympathy Rule—*Rule 40*—applies to written advocacy. Everything we have examined involves *giving sympathy* to our reader, making our presentation as easy and comfort-giving as possible. The rule, you remember, is that the best way of getting sympathy is to give it out.

In our body language advocacy (where we have been *in pro per*, representing ourselves) we have persuaded our reader to meet us with respect and attention. As she begins to read, she is immediately drawn in. It's a little while before she realizes how *good* the writing is and how different from what she usually has to read. She is borne along at exactly the right pace and she finds the story fascinating.

Why? Because you have sifted through all the practical rules of advocacy, wondering which of them does and doesn't apply when it comes to writing. And those great branch rules, the core seven truths, are here with us in the silence of our room, just as they are in court.

Honest Guide—*Rule 44*

Newton—*Rule 41*

Be Likeable—*Rule 39*

Entertain Them—*Rule 21*

Tell Them a Story—*Rule 22*

Be Brief—*Rule 28*

Show Them the Way Home—*Rule 56*

Remember these, and you'll have no difficulty in holding your reader's attention. Nor will you have any difficulty in presenting your arguments as irresistibly as possible. When you have found the Honest Way of presenting your case, present it in accordance with the rules which are now becoming part of you. If you do, you'll be as irresistible on paper as you will be in court.

I'm not going to discuss the rules of English usage, rules like keeping subjects close to their verbs, preferring the active to the passive voice, minimizing your use of negatives, avoiding the use of three words when one will do, etc. There are already excellent books on the subject.

Instead, I leave you with just two thoughts.

First, that awesome statistic about the Grand Canyon. Who calculated it, I don't know, but I've heard it several times: the lawyers of America—over 700,000 of us at the time of writing—could put *seven* layers of paper on the walls of the Grand Canyon in the time it takes the Earth to orbit the Sun.

Remember:

Rule 99

There's No Rule of Court Which Requires Your Document to Be of a Minimum Length

It's the same all the way through advocacy: *brevity works wonders.* If you believe nothing else you have read in this book, believe this.

Brevity is *such* a scarce commodity, now as over the centuries. Listen to one of the greatest of our predecessors, an attorney who used to spellbind juries and whose economic use of English is still an example to us all, but who on this occasion was suffering at the hands of the wordy and the unfocused. Abraham Lincoln, reading a report of a Congressional committee on a new gun, raised his weary head and exclaimed,

> "I should want a new lease of life to read this through! Why can't an investigating committee show a grain of common sense? If I

send a man to buy a horse for me, I expect him to tell me that horse's points—not how many hairs he has in his tail!"

Why can't an attorney show a grain of common sense, and regard it as a point of professional honor to be as brief as possible? We have already turned up a number of reasons—the sheer weight of tradition and convention, the occasional need for the precision of the engineer, the badge-language we are tempted to flaunt—but there is another reason, a much more sinister one, and it is this.

Churning out boilerplate makes money.

A battalion of associates busily producing needless verbiage not only pays the rent, it makes a handsome profit.

I recently received a 72-page document. It was the answer to some interrogatories in a wrongful termination case. Every single interrogatory had first been objected to, then answered briefly. The objection occupied seven lines, and the identical seven lines had been reproduced, over and over again, in respect of every single request.

It was a wearisome reading. It involved trudging from page to page, wading through repetitious junk to find the meat of the response. Three words were all we needed: "The same objection." Everyone would have understood and not one of us would have complained about the missing seven lines. Two-thirds of the paper would have been saved.

And it was slightly sickening to reflect that this cynical waste of paper, time, and effort is how our profession operates. Those answers to interrogatories were absolutely typical: the generating of useless language is *the norm*. It pays the rent.

That pleading came from a law firm that enjoys the highest reputation. All their other pleadings have been the same. When they took my client's deposition, they spun it out over nine days.

We all know what I'm talking about. This shameless behavior is rampant in the legal profession. And it's not only done to make money: there's a grubbier motive some of the time.

It is a recognized strategy, these days, to paper your opponent to death. Drown him. Use up his resources. Wage a war of attrition. Use the financial muscle of your client to drive your opponent into the ground. Beat him, not on the justice of the case, or on the right interpretation of law and fact, but by superior wealth.

There are hordes of American attorneys willing to sell themselves as mercenaries in this shabby war.

Take another look in the mirror. Are you one of them?

If your client objects to paying as much for a slender document as he would pay for half a pound of wasted paper, use a little private advocacy. Remind him of what Mark Twain wrote to Abigail—when he apologized for the length of his letter, explaining that it would have been much shorter if he had had more time.

Remind your client, too, that the slow process of distillation which makes brandy out of wine has its counterpart in lawyering, and that ten words that move your reader are worth more than ten thousand that don't. Show him your product and explain the work that went into it. Explain, as you explained before you began your trial, that brevity is your secret weapon, but that it has to be worked for with time and effort. Do this, and you're unlikely to have trouble with your bill.

Brevity is not only a characteristic of effective advocacy. In this profession of ours it is a badge of honor, recognized as such by the oppressed judges and by every thoughtful attorney. You want to be outstanding? Be brief.

Lastly, a reference back to the Video Dimension. Just think about this: every time you create a document, you are producing something that might be used in evidence.

If a dispute arises and litigation ensues, your creation may well find itself up there, on the screen of an overhead projector, in front of a critically attentive jury, being carefully ripped apart by a skillful Honest Guide.

Think before you begin to write, think as you write, and think as you put your name to your finished product; think of that rather sobering possibility.

Bear these practical guidelines in mind from first to last and your words will always be worth the paper they are written on.

CHAPTER TWELVE

Advocacy in the Age of High Technology

Very few attorneys ever have the privilege of arguing a case in the Supreme Court of the United States. Those who do are presented with a white quill pen. One of my colleagues got his recently, framed it, and hung it on his wall just above the desk where his computer stands.

If you look into it, you discover that the time interval between quill pen and personal computer is hardly more than a hundred years. Modern times, for the lawyer, started in the 1870s. Remington, the gunsmiths, began marketing typewriters in 1873, three years before Bell patented the first telephone, and four years before Edison patented the ancestor of the dictating machine. It was as recently as 1908, the year when mass-production of the automobile began, that the fountain pen suddenly caught on. Only eighty years later, personal computers were everywhere. This explosion of technology has all happened very, very quickly.

How swiftly the legal profession accommodated and is accommodating to this rapid change, I don't know. I do know that the English barristers were still arguing in the 1970s that they didn't need photo-copying machines, and that some lawyers in the 1990s still hadn't discovered the incalculable usefulness of the personal computer.

But advocacy from now on can't afford *not* to be abreast of the times. This is because there *are* advocates who have grasped the possibilities of high technology. If you ignore these possibilities and come up against an opponent who has the latest tools and knows how to use them, you could find yourself at an overwhelming disadvantage.

Every advocate or aspiring advocate ought to be aware of the technology that is already with us and that which is to come. I emphasize that this is written by one who practiced for twenty-five years under the old conditions, before realizing that it is not only essential for us to understand this technological revolution—it is also fun. Some of the tools now available are exciting as well as immensely useful.

Do regard it as important to stay in the know about what's available as the latest new tool. Most judges are convinced computers speed things up. They permit computers and video into their courtrooms and it's not likely that they'll start restricting them. This means that in not many years from now, trial advocacy will have acquired a new dimension.

Imagine cross-examining an expert.

"Now, Dr. Brodschatzer, you've just given us the principal numbers you relied on?"
"Yes."

"Let's put them up, so the jury can see them. Why don't we turn them into a chart?"

And there, with the jury watching it all on their screen, you call up the pie-chart program, plug in the expert's figures as they watch, make the occasional slip and have to correct it, just as in real life, pick the colors, and press *Enter*. There on your jury's screen appears the pie chart, created in front of them. And they watched, over your shoulder, as you created it. They did so with all the fascination of people watching something *interesting*.

I suspect that computer dexterity may become a powerful tool under the Entertain Them Rule. Showing the jury exactly how you get there as you rivet them into the Video Dimension underscores your status as Honest Guide. And never forget those statistics: they'll remember 10 percent of what they hear, but they'll retain 50 percent of what they *see* and hear.

Come, lastly, to a much more homely tool:

Video

More than ten years ago, I watched a 20-minute video that had been made for a settlement conference. It was a day in the life of the plaintiff. She was quadriplegic. In an ecological case I did some time back, I showed the jury video that had been shot from a helicopter. The pattern of damage was unarguable. An edited video of a deposition can be the most devastating instrument of impeachment. The in-court use of video, rare when I wrote the first edition of this book, is now commonplace.

Videos usually speak for themselves.

Since they have to be created by experts—only use homemade video as an *absolute* last resort—they are expensive to produce, and they tend to be used mainly in the bigger claims. But if the case justifies the expense, don't pass up the chance of using a video.

People often focus more intently on a screen than on real life. We humans have a very wide field of vision, and we expend more energy than we realize just filtering out irrelevant background information. If that background noise and static is filtered out for us, and we are invited to focus on a comfortable screen, we do so willingly. Anything you can frame with a screen will get focused attention.

This blossoming of technology that is going on all round us has narrowed the gap between the senior, experienced advocate and the more recent arrival in the profession. The young are clever at using technology. It could be that a whole new style of advocacy may arise, in which the hero-lawyer is a bespectacled, serious young computer geek with a wry smile. All he does all the way through the case is *show them the way home* as he takes them on their fascinating journey.

I hope I never have him as my opponent.

A final practical rule, therefore, to guide the trial advocate must be this:

Rule 100
Stay Abreast of Technological Advances

Conclusion

Enough, then, and over to you. If you truly resolve to be one of the *real* advocates of your time, that is almost certainly what you will become. If you do as I suggested at the beginning of this book, and continue to spend ten minutes every day reading a little and thinking a little about advocacy, then, shameful though it is to realize it, you will be doing much more than most of your competitors.

We've looked together at exactly a hundred practical rules, most of which represent potential traps you might have fallen into. You're not likely to do that now, but I'll tell you what you *are* going to do.

From now on, when you go into court, you are going to be infinitely more aware of how your contemporaries are performing. You are going to watch, probably with fascination, the extent to which these rules are broken—in every court and on every day when the courts are sitting. And you are going to *know* exactly what is being done wrong. You'll also know what is being done right, and you'll recognize really good advocacy as soon as you see it.

As I said early on, simply by being aware of these sensible rules, you'll improve as an advocate. More than that, you'll improve rapidly. The secret is those two or three minutes every day—you don't need more—of glancing at the rules, followed up with seven or eight minutes, some time during the next twenty-four hours, musing about advocacy. Your self-confidence will grow quickly because you'll see the results, and the more acutely you are aware of the rules, the more you will find yourself putting them into effect. You will become an Honest Guide, a skillful, persuasive advocate—and you are sorely needed.

You are needed because the world we live in is moving into history's most critical phase, and, faced with the pressures of these dangerous and difficult times, the leaders of humankind are likely to be more and more tempted to side-step and override the rule of law. It always happens when the going gets tough, and the going is already getting tough.

If liberty, justice and the rule of law are to be saved and upheld, it is you and others like you who must save and uphold them. We are arriving at a time in human affairs when the truth is likely to come into conflict with doublespeak and dogma even more than usual, and the role of the honest and courageous advocate is going to be a vitally important one.

More, even, than that, we are now inhabiting a world that is interconnected to a degree undreamed of in other times. There is a wild, democratic impulse sweeping the planet and, thanks to the Internet, satellites, screens, and fax machines, everyone can watch and take sides as people everywhere struggle to tame the unruly beast we call democracy. There has never before been such a need, nor such an opportunity, for enlightened, skillful advocates to argue and explain and persuade.

Advocacy, honest advocacy, is about making people see the truth with a new awareness. It is about persuading people to follow this course rather than that one. All you have to do, today, is look around and you see the need for enlightenment, the need for new and different priorities, the need for completely new attitudes and actions. The question is: will they be brought about by force or by persuasion? Force has had a long and bloody innings, and we are all too dangerously be-weaponed to place too much faith in force.

That leaves persuasion. It could be that we are entering the Age of the Honest Advocate.

As I say, you are needed.

Good luck.

Why Color Is Critical

What follows is a much-abridged version of an article appearing in the *California Law Practice Management* journal by Gloria Boileau, a color and image consultant. I first encountered Ms. Boileau's teaching at a National Institute of Trial Advocacy seminar. I was surprised and alarmed by her message, and arranged for her to come and talk to our firm. So impressive was her presentation that she was invited back, not once but three times, so as to reach all our support staff as well as attorneys.

I had heard that studies had been done on the subliminal impact of color, but I knew nothing about the results of such studies, I had never seen any demonstrations, and I approached the whole subject with guarded cynicism. Ms. Boileau left us in no doubt about the reality, and the importance, of the discoveries made in this field.

Since being aware of the theoretical impact of color, I've been noticing how color is used, both in and out of the courtroom. As you might expect, the retail industry understands color and uses it to tremendous effect. We lawyers, on the other hand, seem almost wholly ignorant of its importance. The advocate who *does* understand color, and who uses it properly, unquestionably steals a lead over the rest of us. Because I now realize how important this is, I am including this material as an appendix.

"Non-verbal communication is six times more powerful than words. . . . Within seven seconds, your audience will decide on your competence and credibility based on the visual image you present. . . .

"Herein lies a fundamental lesson that law schools do not teach—for your case to succeed, you, your clients, and your witnesses must look trustworthy and behave credibly. [You can] heighten your . . . credibility through the effective use of the subliminal messages conveyed by your attire and by your behavior.

"Color has a major psychological impact on all of us. . . . Studies show that color is the first thing the brain perceives when viewing anything . . . .

"In the last 360 years, there have been only four color systems. The first . . . was Newton's in 1660, followed by Munsell's in 1880 and Oswald's in 1900. All of these systems . . . were (either the result of pure research or were) directed at the professional artist and designer.

"The most recent system, developed in 1950 by Dr. Robert Dorr . . . teaches you how to use color personally and professionally. Dr. Dorr, a graduate of the Chicago Academy of Fine Arts, discovered the . . . meaning of *pigment-relationship*. In his years as an artist and designer, he found that *all colors contain undertones of either blue or yellow pigmentation*. For example, when you look at two shades of the color red, one might be very bright (fire-engine red) and the other might be much deeper (the shade of a dark cherry). The difference between these two colors is their base pigmentation. The bright red has a yellow base . . . while the deep red has a blue base pigmentation.

"When colors of blue base pigmentation are combined together, the result creates a feeling of harmony. The same is true when yellow-pigmented colors are combined. Yet when blue-pigmented colors are combined with yellow-pigmented colors the result creates discord and is unpleasant to the viewer.

". . . Dr. Dorr . . . observed that not only colors, but *people also have inherent undertone of either blue or yellow pigmentation in their skin, eyes and hair. . . .* [His] findings were validated with 100% accuracy after testing thousands of individuals at Stanford, USC and UCLA. . . . All color research was validated by a General Electric recording spectro-photometer.

"Realizing that each of us has a spectrum of color which is ideally suited to our own natural coloring it is important to stay within that spectrum. For example, when blue-pigmented individuals wear blue-pigmented colors, they . . . look healthy, alive, rich and energetic, and convey a subliminal message of harmony, balance, and strength. If . . . the same people dress in yellow-pigmented colors, they convey a look of discord, disorder, sallowness and poor health.

"Scientists are looking more and more into the power of color and the way it works. They have evidence that color affects blood pressure, respiration, eye movement, body temperature, mood, and glandular activity. These effects are subconscious and uncontrollable.

"Color emits its own form of energy as an . . . electromagnetic wave . . . that penetrates the body. When these waves reach the pineal and pituitary glands, their effect is reflected through the entire body. These findings were borne out by Alexander Schauss at the American Institute of Biological Research in Tacoma, Washington, who did experiments with blind people. He discovered that the blind responded to color and can "see" it mentally. . . . Color has definite power over the human mind and body and we will be affected differently depending on the colors we are viewing.

"Navy blue signifies truth and wisdom. It is the most acceptable color to all classes and is an outstanding favorite throughout the world. Thus you should wear it when you want to appeal to a more general audience. Black conveys very strong authority and power. It often intimidates . . . unless it is softened by another color. White is emotionally negative, as it is perceived as bleak and sterile. White needs to be balanced with another color that has a more pleasing impact. Beige and light tan are not high statement colors and will cause you to blend into the background. Red is perhaps the most dominant and dynamic of all colors . . . and increases the nervous tension that creates action. Red can be very effective when you want to make a critical point that will get a response. . . . Vivid pink, on the other hand, causes the glands to slow the secretion of adrenaline, thereby relaxing the heart and body muscles. Yellow is considered energizing and stimulates learning especially when used in its clearest, brightest tone. Green is a balancing color, especially if it is a grass green color. It reduces nervous and muscular tension. Generally, orange is not preferred in its pure form, but it is highly pleasing in its tints such as peach or salmon."

Common Sense Rules of Advocacy for Lawyers at a Glance

The Dimensions

1. You must dress appropriately. *(Page 10)*
2. Don't be seen in too friendly a relationship with your opponent. *(Page 11)*
3. Don't smile, laugh, or joke without including the jury in. *(Page 12)*
4. Appear at all times to be absolutely sincere. *(Page 12)*
5. Never convey any visual signal you do not intend to convey. *(Page 12)*
6. Ensure that your factfinder always has something to look at. *(Page 13)*
7. Use all kinds of visual aids. *(Page 13)*
8. Maintain eye contact with the factfinder. *(Page 15)*
9. Stick rigorously to the truth. *(Page 17)*
10. Don't appear to be manipulative. *(Page 18)*

11. Don't sound like a lawyer. *(Page 18)*

12. Don't repeat yourself. *(Page 21)*

The Mandatory Rules

13. In opening statement, avoid all argument and stick strictly to facts. *(Page 24)*

14. Be sure, in opening statement, to state enough facts to justify the verdict you are asking for. *(Page 26)*

15. The advocate must not express his or her opinion in court. *(Page 27)*

16. As an advocate, never give or appear to give evidence yourself. *(Page 31)*

17. Never refer to the record of an accused person or to any offers of settlement. *(Page 32)*

18. Never put words into the mouth of your own witness. *(Page 33)*

19. In your closing argument, speak only of things that have been touched upon in the evidence. *(Page 35)*

Advocacy as Theater

20. Commit to being an excellent trial lawyer. Don't do anything by halves. If you can't dedicate yourself to this, move over and do something else. *(Page 40)*

21. Entertain them. *(Page 44)*

22. Tell them a story. *(Page 45)*

23. Think beginning, middle, and end. *(Page 46)*

The Psychology of Advocacy

44. Always aim to be the honest guide. *(Page 75)*

45. Don't ask the factfinder to believe the unbelievable. *(Page 76)*

46. Where there is a weak point in your case, don't pretend it isn't a weak point. *(Page 76)*

47. Don't misquote the evidence or put a slick interpretation on any part of it. *(Page 76)*

48. Make sure you come across as being absolutely fair. *(Page 77)*

49. Keep your objections to a minimum. *(Page 77)*

50. Take great care getting your jury out of court for bench conferences. *(Page 78)*

51. Demonstrate your competence to your judge as early as possible. *(Page 79)*

52. Practice listening intently. *(Page 80)*

53. Stop dead in your tracks as soon as you realize your sentence has become too complicated. *(Page 80)*

54. There must be an overall theme to your case, and you should be able to tell the story in one compact sentence. *(Page 83)*

55. The planning rule—in three parts. *(Page 85)*

56. Show them the way home. *(Page 87)*

The Examination of Witnesses

57. Think out in advance the answer you want to hear, and design your questions with a view to getting that precise answer. *(Page 97)*

58. Every examination should consist of a series of objectives. *(Page 101)*

59. Never forget that the average witness speaks from memory. *(Page 105)*

60. Never forget, you are not dealing with facts, but with what the witness believes to be facts. *(Page 106)*

61. Go gently when you attack a witness's recollection. *(Page 107)*

62. Never turn to a witness for help. *(Page 107)*

63. The one line of transcript rule. *(Page 108)*

64. Don't ask compound questions. *(Page 109)*

65. Use variety in the format of your questions. *(Page 109)*

66. Beware of demanding the Yes or No answer. *(Page 110)*

Direct Examination

67. The Foundation Rule: Before you may ask a witness to testify on any topic, you must lay a foundation showing how the witness has acquired knowledge of that topic. *(Page 117)*

68. In direct examination, remember the Rule of Two and couple your questions wherever you can. *(Page 118)*

Cross-Examination

69. Stop when you get what you want. *(Page 135)*

70. Use leading questions in cross-examination. *(Page 135)*

71. Pin down the witness: don't spring the trap until the witness is inside. *(Page 137)*

72. Keep the record as favorable to you as possible by moving to strike any inadmissible evidence. *(Page 139)*

73. Ride the bumps: keep your dismay secret. *(Page 141)*

74. The minefield rule: never jump back in alarm. *(Page 142)*

75. Don't cross-examine at all unless you have to. *(Page 143)*

76. Don't go fishing. *(Page 144)*

77. Don't ask questions to which you don't know the answer. *(Page 145)*

78. Never ask "Why?" and never ask "How?" *(Page 146)*

79. Don't open the door. *(Page 146)*

80. Don't let the witness repeat her direct testimony. *(Page 147)*

81. Don't ever get into an argument with a witness. *(Page 148)*

82. Don't ask the fatal final question. *(Page 148)*

Re-Direct

83. If you don't do re-direct well, it's better you don't do it at all. Re-direct must be done confidently and effortlessly. *(Page 155)*

Final Argument

84. It's the factfinder's emotion, not yours, that matters. *(Page 162)*

85. Emotion follows facts and not the other way around. *(Page 162)*

86. Too little emotion is fatal: too much emotion is fatal. *(Page 163)*

87. Acknowledge the feelings that have understandably been stirred up. *(Page 164)*

Written Advocacy

88. Lawyers use far too much paper. *(Page 169)*

89. Good legal writing is easy to read and interesting, accomplishing its goal in as few words as possible. *(Page 174)*

90. The appearance of your document is vitally important. *(Page 177)*

91. White space is user-friendly. *(Page 178)*

92. Don't produce a paragraph deeper than four inches. *(Page 178)*

93. Margins have an effect on the reader. *(Page 179)*

94. Lists of more than three items should be vertical, not horizontal. *(Page 179)*

95. Use headings. *(Page 182)*

96. Consider incorporating diagrams into your writing. *(Page 182)*

97. Write at the pace of a brisk walk. *(Page 185)*

98. Pay great respect to chronology in your writing. *(Page 187)*

99. There's no rule of court requiring a document to be of a minimum length. *(Page 191)*

Lastly

100. Stay abreast of technological advances. *(Page 199)*

How to Succeed as a Lawyer

By Roland Boyd

More than forty years ago, attorney Roland Boyd of McKinney, Texas, wrote a letter to his son offering tips on how to be a successful lawyer. When several Texas State Bar officials saw the letter, they prevailed upon the elder Boyd to allow the Texas Bar Journal *to print it. Boyd agreed and it appeared in the November 1962 issue.*

Dear Son:

You are now in your senior year in law school. Maybe a few things I have learned in thirty years in the law practice will be helpful. Law school is teaching you things which will be good for your clients; the following will be good for you. You cannot have professional happiness unless you are financially successful.

One of the greatest pleasures in life is achievement. In my judgment, if you will remember the following twenty-one things, you will have a long, happy, and successful career.

Reprinted with permission of William M. Boyd and from the *Texas Bar Journal*.

1. Remember the rule of nine.

It works this way: nine people out of ten are good, honest, intelligent, decent, and fair-minded people. Therefore, if you want to have the odds, nine to one, in your favor, get on the right side of the issue. In the legal profession, the right side of the issue is the side that helps society. In other words, don't injure your fellow man. In the courtroom the rule of nine works the same way. Nine times out of ten the right side wins at the courthouse. But, I believe that the lawyers in the smaller county seat cities engaging in the general practice of civil law are more convinced that the rule of nine really works than the average city lawyers.

2. Remember, a lawyer's integrity is of vital concern to the community.

If the butcher, the baker, and the candlestick maker are not honest, this is not a major catastrophe. But on the other hand, the lawyer plays such a vital role in the lives of his fellow men that if he is not honest, it is a major catastrophe. Let me give you some examples of the vital roles a lawyer is called on to play:

(a) A few years ago, shortly after noon in July, the door to my private office opened; there stood a man, a little past middle age. I had represented him for many years; he was a successful farmer; he was very pale, and was trembling all over as he said, "I have just made the worst mistake a man can possibly make. I have killed a man, I knew a second after it was done how terrible it was. For God's sake, help me."

(b) About ten years ago, three members of a family, two others of whom had just had visited upon them one of the most horrible crimes that had ever occurred in Texas, came to my office. This family was face-to-face with stark, unnatural tragedy. The spokesman said, "At a family meeting this morning we all agreed that we wanted you as special prosecutor, to help us see that justice is done."

(c) A few weeks ago, an elderly retired farmer, a good, sound citizen, came to the office bringing with him a smartly and attractively dressed daughter, apparently about 35 years old. He told me a story of the daughter's marriage to an energetic, handsome, well-educated, dynamic young man, how well he was doing in business, how the family began growing, and then embezzlement, then divorce, then a new life, then remarriage, then robbery with firearms and murder, now a death penalty in just a day or so. "We need your help."

(d) Several months ago, on a Saturday afternoon, while I was in the office with the outside doors locked, a telephone call from a middle-aged man I had represented for years, as well as his father before him, in a distressed voice, said, "I am downstairs, your door is locked, but I was just praying that you were in. I must talk to you." When he arrived, he showed me several daily newspapers that he had just gotten out of the post office from a distant city. The headlines and front-page articles told a story of a liquor store stickup with the owner being murdered when he tried to reach for a gun, the capture by police blockade, the laboratory reports proving conclusively who had fired the shot that killed the owner. His son. Crying like a baby, the man said: "Help me. What can I do?"

(e) You might be employed by the State Bar of Texas to investigate, brief, file, and try a fellow lawyer in a disbarment proceeding. This assignment cannot be taken lightly.

(f) In thirty years of practicing law I have felt that my professional duty required me to ask a jury to take a man's life on three different occasions. In two cases, the jury complied with my request; in the third, the defendant took his own life the day he was sentenced for life. Under these conditions the only reward life provides is a clear conscience. No profession can be more vital than one which makes such requirements on its members. Therefore, the integrity of its members is certainly of major concern to society.

3. Remember, always be nice to people regardless of their social status, educational level, or financial rating.

(a) That boy who is now "jerking soda" at the drugstore, twenty-five years from now might be president of the Investment Bankers Association of America and calling you about an important matter in New York.

(b) That boy who is now picking up scrap metal in the alleys and selling it to get spending money, twenty years hence might be employing you to examine titles to ranch lands he is buying in other states.

(c) That boy, who, on graduation from high school, said, "I am not going to college because I already have all the education I need," might many years hence, by being elected chairman of the board of directors of a major manufacturing concern, prove the truth of his statement.

(d) Some successful people in business can neither read nor write.

4. Remember, in the practice of law under a democratic form of government there are no secrets.

Therefore, don't ever be a party to anything, don't put anything in a letter, don't say anything in conference or on the telephone that you would mind (except for your client's interest) seeing on the front page of a newspaper, on TV, or hearing from the witness stand, or on the radio.

5. Remember, the best way to disarm your enemies is to do what is just under the circumstances.

It absolutely drives them crazy. Often it will throw them into such confusion that they become helpless. Ordinarily their "double-dealing" will "backfire" if you don't resort to the same tactics.

6. Remember, no people have ever developed a better method for settling disputes among men than our judicial system.

It was developed by the legal profession, and it has been through fire millions of times; although not perfect, it is still the best there is. The jury is the heart of the system. Always defend the system. When you lose a lawsuit, don't try to tear the courthouse down.

7. Remember, the important thing, so far as getting legal business is concerned, is what your homefolks think about you.

Everything on earth connects to your town and then your block. How high you go in your profession depends on who employs you.

The important employment I have had in many different matters which has necessitated my being out of the state much of the time can be traced back to someone very close to home. So it is what your neighbors say about you that counts.

8. Remember, no profession makes it possible for its members to enjoy a longer professional life than law.

So long as a lawyer lives he can practice law. So long as he keeps his health and mind he can do it successfully. Our neighbor, the late senator, demonstrated this fact; he practiced law for seventy years.

9. Remember, there is no ceiling on success in the legal profession.

The only limits on the amount of success you can achieve are your time and energy. And the thought that will give strength to finish when the hour gets late and going gets rough is that, irrespective of how it might look to others, you know you are fighting according to the accepted rules of the game.

10. Remember, the end does not justify the means.

Two wrongs do not make a right. It is better to lose than not to fight according to the rules. It is extremely easy for a young lawyer to violate these rules. If you have a growing family to support on a meager income, there is a strong temptation to become lax on your professional morals. Many times it might appear necessary to "fudge" a little. You will profit financially if you don't do it. The magnitude of responsibility entrusted to you is in direct proportion to the confidence people have in you. No one can destroy the confidence of other people in you, except you. Integrity is key; therefore, you must not only be honest, but also you must maintain the appearance of honesty.

11. Remember, to be a good lawyer you must first be a good man.

Your sole ambition should be to be a good husband, a good father, a good neighbor, a good citizen, and a good lawyer. If you achieve this, you will have achieved all the success there is. The pressure of life. In the space age, it is very easy for a young man to get the idea that he must be a dynamic individual, he must break all records, he must set the world on fire. If he gets this idea, he starts life with a handicap. The papers are full of such cases at this time.

12. Remember, don't ever put your interest in the fee ahead of your interest in the case.

Your future depends more on the manner in which you handle the case than on the amount of the fee you collect.

13. Remember, the primary purpose of the legal profession is to find, recognize, interpret, and preserve the truth.

The quicker you can learn the truth about any situation, the better off you will be. After you learn it, don't join issue against it.

14. Remember, your clients subconsciously make you the guardian of their morals.

As inconspicuously as possible you should assume this responsibility. If you do, and discharge it properly, it will help you build a good law practice:

(a) Many years ago a client who lived in a nearby city came to the office and said, "That case you are representing me in, I got to thinking, that property represents 90 percent of my life's work. If you lose that case, I am ruined. A man told me if I would go to so and so and pay him $10,000, then my property would be reappraised at a high figure and I could settle without a trial. I have about decided to do it that way. What do you think?" I told him in my opinion he would be making the greatest mistake he had ever made; that he had always been honest and I couldn't see any reason for him to change this late in life. He reluctantly agreed. A few months later, he was well pleased with the outcome of his case, and told me many times that I kept him from ruining a happy and successful life. He consulted me on every important matter for the balance of his life.

(b) A few years ago, about mid-morning, I got a call from a local citizen who was then in a distant city. He made an appointment as soon as he could drive. That afternoon, when he arrived, he explained that he had been low bidder on a big construction contract, that the second bidder had approached him on the proposition that if he did not qualify, the second bidder would be awarded the contract, then he would let him do the work and they would split the difference in the two bids. He wanted me to write a contract that would bind both parties. After explaining why no lawyer could write that contract without committing a felony, he decided to qualify and perform, which he did. He and his entire family have been my clients since then.

15. Remember, the courtroom is where the showdown comes.

This is where the lawyer must "put up or shut up." This is the arena in which you must meet your adversary. There is a large segment of the profession who avoid the courtroom in every possible manner. This is a mistake. Of course, the courtroom is strictly the last resort, but I never had any luck in handling matters in negotiation until I got the situation in good shape for the courtroom. If you have a good case and are well prepared, nine times out of ten you don't have to try it. If you are not well prepared, you will either lose the case or coerce your client into an unfair settlement. Trial work is essential for the general practitioner; until you have a fair estimate of what you can or can't do at the courthouse, you have no true standard by which to measure your case. The trial lawyer is to the legal profession what the surgeon is to the medical profession. An office lawyer who never goes into the courtroom never knows whether he is rendering the right kind of service to his clients. To be a good "trial lawyer" you must know why, where, when, and how people "tick." The highest compliment that can be paid a lawyer is to say, "He is a good trial lawyer."

16. Remember, there is no sure way to bind men together and keep them bound by any written instrument.

The only thing that binds men together is the fact that under all circumstances most men, without knowing what the other will do, will reach for the golden rope of justice, truth, decency, and fairness, and thereby bind themselves to every other person who grasps the same rope. This is the only combine that will endure.

17. Remember to live for your fiftieth birthday.

Soon after I graduated and opened my office, one of the service clubs had as guest speaker an evangelist who was holding a revival in a big tent on the trade lot. In his talk, he said: "I don't care what your life's work is; if you are a young man just beginning, I am going to tell you what to expect from life. If from now until your fiftieth birthday you will make every decision in your business or profession in such a way as you think helps society, from your fiftieth birthday on, for the balance of your life, the pleasure you get from your life's work will double every twelve months. On the other hand, if your decisions are against society, your disappointments and your miseries will double every twelve months." I am now three years past my fiftieth birthday. I believe the man was right.

18. Remember, money loses most of its importance when you get sufficient food, clothing, and shelter for you and your family.

And at this point, with most people, the pleasure diminishes as the amount increases. People who have nothing but money have very little.

**19. Remember that the happiest man on earth is
the man who has to work for a living.**

**20. Remember that many of your thrills, excitement,
unusual experiences, etc., will come in peculiar fashion
and at unexpected times.**

(a) A call from an undertaker saying the funeral has started, that
he is calling for one of the mourners who asked that you not accept
employment from anyone else until he could get to your office after
the funeral.

(b) While walking to the office just at sun-up during the middle
of a long, vicious trial, on coming to an intersection, seeing a man
standing in the middle of the walk, with no other human being in
sight, who three days before said he was going to whip you, on
account of your role in the trial.

(c) The woman who drove twenty miles, rushed into your office,
and said, "I just heard you died of a heart attack. Thank God it
wasn't true."

(d) On driving up to a filling station, the owner, whom you don't
remember ever having seen before, saying to a child: "Honey, go get
your mother; this man talked us out of getting a divorce many years
ago. We both want to thank him."

(e) Clients who send more than their fee, and say you didn't
charge them enough (this doesn't happen often, but it gives you a
thrill when it does).

(f) Thank you letters from distant heirs that you have never
met.

(g) People coming to your office as new clients, whom you have previously sued.

21. Remember that the people who stay hitched the longest usually fare the best.

I believe you have the ability to succeed in medicine, engineering, business, or almost anything you might want to undertake, but you don't have the time. To become thoroughly qualified, to establish yourself, and to succeed in any line requires an entire lifetime. So the people who chart a course early in life and stay with it are usually the ones who enjoy the greatest success. In the legal profession this same principle applies to location. Many times each month, people come to my office as a result of some association with them or other members of the family several years ago. If you don't stay put in one spot, you lose this advantage.

I believe that after you have practiced law for thirty years, you too, will know that law is the greatest profession there is.

Sincerely,
Your Father

Index

References are to page numbers.
References to Rules appear in parentheses, e.g., (R 39).

F

Face and facial expression, 10
Fair, always appear to be, (R48), 77
Feelings, 163-166
Final argument,
    Generally, 160-166
    In civil defense case, 164
    In criminal case, 71-72
First Dimension of Advocacy, 6-7, 64, 146
First Person Plural—Rule of, (R 42), 73
Fishing, don't go, (R 76), 144
Flogging the trivial point, 131
Footnotes, wage war on, 186
Forehead, 10
Forms of questions, 109
Foundation Rule, 115-122
Fountain pen, 196
Fourth Dimension, 19-22
Freight train cars, 101-102

G

Get him to commit himself, 138
Go gently when you attack a witness's recollection, (R 61), 107
Good legal writing is easy to read, (R 89), 174
Grand Canyon, 169, 191
Grunt, nod, or shake of the head, 34

H

Headings, (R 95), 182
Hearing is believing, 8

Hemingway, Ernest, 48
High technology, 196-199
Hollywood, 38
"Home", 87
Honest Guide, (R 44), 75-79, 111, 194
Honesty, 7, 75
How? and What? questions in direct examination, 115, 117

I

If you don't do re-direct well, it's better you don't do it at all, (R 83), 155
"Ignored her to death—twice!", 84
Iliad, 185
Imitation, no need for, 41
In pari delicto, 18
In the hills and dales of Killarney, 19
Include the factfinder in, (R 42), 73
Inconsistency of testimony, 137
Individuality, 41
Insecurity, 21
Interpretation of perception, 105
Invite, don't demand, 70
Irresistible advocacy, 102

J

Johnson, Dr. Samuel, 16
Joking, 12
Jury box, getting close to, 59
Jury not a committee of inquiry, 6
Jury out of court during bench conferences, 78

Plan your approach to the witness stand, (R 37), 60

Planning, 52, 85-86, 102

Plumed helmet, 172, 180

Police are the good guys, 71-72

Polyester, 10

Practice listening intently, (R 52), 80

Preferences and opinions, 64, 65

Preparation, 41, 42, 85-86, 101-103

Prepare them, (R 43), 74

Prepare them for the boring bits, (R 29), 54

Presentation designed to persuade, 7

Private advocacy, 21

Psychology of advocacy, 64-93

Pulling strings, 98

Q

Questions,
    Correct forms of, 109
    Fatal, final, 148-152
    Paired, 118-122
    To which you don't know the answer, 145
    Use variety in the form of, (R 65), 109

Quill pen, 197

R

Railroad freight train, 101, 102

Raising your voice, 57

Reagan, Ronald, 66

Real, being, 67

Recollection, 105-107

Record, keep it favorable, (R 72), 139

Re-direct, 154-157

Remingtons, 196

Repetition, 21-22, 81-82

Resentment, 20, 35, 50

Ride the bumps, (R 73), 141

Right, where before there was wrong, 88

Robbins, Harold, 48

Rogers, Will, 16

Rule of Law, 203

Running in harness with jurors, 73

Rules

Acknowledge the feelings that have understandably stirred up (Rule 87), 164

Aim to create sympathy between you and your factfinder (Rule 40), 67

Always aim to be the honest guide (Rule 44), 75

Always aim to maintain your continuity (Rule 24), 46

Appear at all times to be absolutely sincere (Rule 4), 12

As an advocate, never give or appear to give evidence yourself (Rule 16), 31

Avoid detail (Rule 26), 50

Be aware of timing and use the power of the pause (Rule 32), 57

Be brief (Rule 28), 52, 134

Be likeable (Rule 39), 66

References are to page numbers.
References to Rules appear in parentheses, e.g., (R 39).

S

References are to page numbers.
References to Rules appear in parentheses, e.g., (R 39).

References are to page numbers.
References to Rules appear in parentheses, e.g., (R 39).

TheCapitol.Net
Exclusive provider of Congressional Quarterly Executive Conferences

Media Relations 101*

For the newer public or government affairs professional, this one-day program will help
you develop the essential skills necessary to deal with the Washington media environment.
Includes practical hands-on exercises, who the media is, how to develop your basic message,
preparing an effective press release and complete media kit, and putting it all together in
a communications plan with a strategy for using the web and distributing the message.
The basics of crisis communication planning will also be covered.

www.MediaRelations101.com

Advanced Media Relations*

For public relations professionals with three to five years' experience and those who want
to refresh their outlook or brush up on their skills. Are your competitive media campaigns
targeting the right audience? Are you tracking and evaluating your media campaigns?
Using the web to its full advantage? In one day, we'll cover these topics and more, including:
creatively pitching to reporters, how to handle a crisis, coordinating and preparing for
interviews, and dealing with the media hog and the media mouse.

www.AdvancedMediaRelations.com

* Course materials for both Media courses include *Media Relations Handbook for Agencies,*
Associations, Nonprofits and Congress, by Brad Fitch, Foreword by Mike McCurry.

Detailed Agendas and Secure Online Registration:
www.TheCapitol.Net   202-678-1600

Exclusive provider of Congressional Quarterly Executive Conferences